TEENAGE COUPLES
COPING WITH REALITY

Other Books by Jeanne Warren Lindsay:

Teenage Couples—Caring, Commitment and Change:
How to Build a Relationship that Lasts
Teens Parenting—Your Baby's First Year
Teens Parenting—The Challenge of Toddlers
Teen Dads: Rights, Responsibilities and Joys
Do I Have a Daddy? A Story About a Single-Parent Child
School-Age Parents: Challenge of Three-Generation Living
Parents, Pregnant Teens and the Adoption Option
Pregnant Too Soon: Adoption Is an Option
Open Adoption: A Caring Option

By Jeanne Lindsay and Jean Brunelli:

Teens Parenting—Your Pregnancy and Newborn Journey
(Available in "regular" [RL 6],
Easier Reading [RL 3], and Spanish editions.)

By Jeanne Lindsay and Sally McCullough:

Teens Parenting—Discipline from Birth to Three

By Jeanne Lindsay and Sharon Rodine:

Teen Pregnancy Challenge, Book One:
Strategies for Change

Teen Pregnancy Challenge, Book Two:
Programs for Kids

By Jeanne Lindsay and Catherine Monserrat:

Adoption Awareness: A Guide for Teachers,
Counselors, Nurses and Caring Others

TEENAGE COUPLES
Coping
with Reality

Dealing with Money,
In-Laws, Babies
and Other Details of Daily Life

Jeanne Warren Lindsay, MA, CFCS

Morning
Glory
Press

Buena Park, California

Teenage Couples—Coping with Reality
is part of a two-book series. The other title is
*Teenage Couples—Caring, Commitment and Change:
How to Build a Relationship that Lasts*

Library of Congress Cataloging-in-Publication Data
Lindsay, Jeanne Warren.
　　Teenage couples. Coping with reality : dealing with money, in-
laws, babies and other details of daily life / Jeanne Warren Lindsay.
　　　　p.　　cm.
　　Includes bibliographical references and index.
　　ISBN 0-930934-87-3 : $15.95. -- ISBN 0-930934-86-5 (pbk.) :
$9.95
　　1. Teenage marriage--Juvenile literature. 2. Family life education--
Juvenile literature. 3. Unmarried couples--Juvenile literature.
[1. Marriage. 2. Family life. 3. Teenage parents.]
I. Title. II. Title: Coping with reality.
HQ799.2.M3L555　1995
306.81'0835--dc20　　　　　　　　　　　　　　　94-36860
　　　　　　　　　　　　　　　　　　　　　　　　　　　CIP
　　　　　　　　　　　　　　　　　　　　　　　　　　　AC

MORNING GLORY PRESS, INC.
6595 San Haroldo Way　　　Buena Park, CA 90620-3748
(714) 828-1998　FAX 714/828-2049
Printed and bound in the United States of America

CONTENTS

Preface   9

Foreword   11

1   Coping with Reality   18

Looking at your reality; Discussing the issues; Impor-
tance of extended family; Life changes, even at home;
Preparing for your own place; Money needs change;
Other realities of living; Importance of self-confidence.

2   Living with Your In-Laws   30

Set up guidelines first; What about the housework?;
Working through the problems; Not enough privacy;
Problems with mom; If you're in the middle; Siblings
need attention, too; Different backgrounds may cause
problems; "It's getting better"; How to move out?

3   Sharing the Tasks of Living   46

Roles are changing; Two essentials: paycheck, housework; One person, two jobs?; Two paychecks preferred;
Problem of housework; Shared roles work.

4   Three Meals a Day—Forever!   60

Who's going to cook?; Learning to cook; Fast foods
often expensive; Different families, different foods;
Dealing with different tastes; Thinking ahead;
Nutrition for good health; Planning your shopping.

5   Dollars Make a Difference   74

Sharing spending responsibility; "I earned it. I'll
spend it"; Handling a checking account; What about
credit cards?; Cutting baby expense; How much
baby food?; Saving money with coupons.

6   Less Stress with a Budget   88

When a budget is necessary; Keep track of expenses; Cutting the costs of living; Making a
budget; Spending plan should suit you both; Present
or future oriented?

7   The Challenge of Finding a Job   100

Do you have a job?; Importance of education;
Finding child care; Help with education; Is welfare
enough?; Learning about special programs; Those
who don't work; Both parents need job skills; Baby
inspires hard work; Setting goals.

8   Pregnancy Brings Change   114

Expect mood swings; He wasn't supportive; Better
the second time; If pregnancy means moving;
Prenatal care is essential; Concerns after delivery;
Childbirth and sexual feelings; This, too, will pass;
Sharing baby care helps.

9   Child-Created Commotion   128

Marriage relationship is primary; Satisfying three
people's needs; Newborns don't spoil; Dad is full
parent, too; Baby needs both parents' attention;
Helping dad feel capable; Good parenting takes
learning; Grandparents get in the act.

10　　**Your Next Baby—When?**　　　142

You have choices; Who's responsible?; Contracep-
tives for women; Depo-Provera okay for nursing
moms; Concern about STDs; AIDS—an incurable
STD; Talking about birth control; If you already
have a baby.

11　　**Donna and Tino—Ten Years Together**　　　154

Pregnancy—Family isn't happy; Living with in-
laws; Education is a must; Setting career goals;
The marriage decision; Jealousy—a little; What
about hitting?; Communication tips; Sharing the
work and the joy; Learning to handle money; The
diaper question; Disciplining together; Keeping the
romance alive.

Appendix　　　169

Interviewee Data　　　171

Marriage Expectations Questionnaire　　　173

Annotated Bibliography　　　183

Index　　　189

Getting married or living with a partner complicates one's life a great deal, whatever the couple's ages. If you're a teenager, you may find even more challenges in developing a loving and lasting relationship.

Money is often a problem—there's seldom enough. Especially if you move out on your own, you'll probably find the money never stretches as far as you'd like.

If you can't live on your own, and you're like many other teenage couples, you'll probably live with your parents or your partner's parents. No matter how wonderful those parents are, it's still likely to be difficult to be somebody's child while you're trying to develop a mature relationship with your partner.

When you're living together, who picks up the socks, who cooks, and who earns the money? These can become major questions. You and your partner may not agree on all these issues. If you or your partner is pregnant, you have many new experiences to handle. After your child is born, you'll have even more challenges.

These day-to-day details of living can create havoc in a
relationship. These are issues you two need to handle as
they arise. Compromise will often be necessary along with
a lot of understanding, caring, and respect for each other.
And that's what this book is all about.

*Teenage Couples—Coping with Reality: Dealing with
Money, In-Laws, Babies and Other Details of Daily Life*
covers, as the title implies, the day-to-day survival issues
teen couples must face. The other title in this series, *Teenage Couples—Caring, Commitment and Change: How to
Build a Relationship that Lasts* deals with personal issues
such as communication, helping love grow, handling
jealousy, and such big problems as drug and alcohol abuse
and partner abuse.

As these issues are discussed in these books, you'll find
a lot of quotes from teens who are married or living with a
partner. A description of the 80 young people I interviewed
is included in the Appendix.

These young people's comments and opinions add a
great deal of reality to both *Teenage Couples* books. Perhaps their experiences will help you and your partner face
the realities in your lives in a way that will help your relationship grow into a caring, loving, and forever partnership.

Jeanne Warren Lindsay
November, 1994

FOREWORD

Teenage couple relationships differ from adult couple relationships in important ways.

First and most obvious is the difference in age and experience. By virtue of their age, young couples are usually less emotionally mature and have less experience of the world than older couples. When a freight-train crisis—a medical emergency, loss of job, or threat of eviction—collides with a teenage couple, they are less likely to have seen it coming or know how to cope with the immediate demands of the situation. They are less likely to be capable of putting the crisis in perspective, getting back on track with their lives, and taking steps to forestall a similar experience in the future.

That being said, it must be admitted that plenty of adult couples are ill-equipped to deal with life's rough spots. Adult couples can be just as inexperienced, naive or foolish as adolescent twosomes. And they can't blame it on their youth.

Adult and adolescent couples often differ in the way that

parenthood fits in their lives. Nearly half of all pregnancies in the United States are unplanned, but teenage couples account for more than their share of unintended pregnancies. When pregnancy comes as an unexpected (although predictable) event, the pregnancy, then parenthood, drives the relationship, forcing the couple to face important issues and major life changes.

It would be better for both teenage and adult couples to think seriously about the demands and responsibilities of parenthood before having children. As Jeanne Warren Lindsay writes in *Teenage Couples: Coping with Reality,* "Choosing to have a baby is a big decision. If you have sexual intercourse without using birth control, that's what you're doing. You're choosing to have a baby."

The conventional wisdom is that more adult couples think they know what they're getting into when they become parents, and more teenage couples are unaware of what parenthood entails. But neither adults nor adolescents are guaranteed to be good or bad parents. Far more important than age is the willingness to work hard at becoming good parents.

By virtue of their age and inexperience, teen couples are economically disadvantaged. Good paying jobs with a strong future are not open to young people who have barely graduated from high school, dropped out, or not yet finished high school. Finishing high school and continuing to improve one's future prospects by more schooling or job training is an important task for young couples. Teenagers may think it is too much to ask when they are struggling to support themselves and maybe a baby as well. But the facts are clear: more education means a better future for young couples and their children.

So, teenage couples are noted for their lack of life experience, more unplanned pregnancies, perhaps an unawareness of what they're getting into, and fewer financial resources at their disposal. But many an adult couple has started life together immature and inexperienced, unaware of what they are about, and without current or future financial stability.

Teenage couple relationships may be most distinctive because of the lack of respect they receive. Relationships between teenagers are often trivialized and dismissed as of little importance.

Adults may believe that adolescents are better off postponing serious relationships, but pretending that young people do not get seriously involved during their teen years is missing the point. Adolescent relationships are not any less important than relationships between adults. Teen couples are dealing with the same strong emotions, the power of sexual attraction and desire, and the important life-long issues of intimacy, commitment and responsibility.

School teachers in Sweden are encouraged to respect and support young people's feelings about the importance of sexual fidelity in relationships. The notion of respecting adolescent couple relationships is not even discussed here in the United States, perhaps because we fear it will encourage these early relationships.

Adults should not trivialize or disrespect teenage couple relationships for the same reasons they should not undermine or make fun of adolescent friendships. Teenage couple relationships that do not extend into adulthood still surely form the basis for future couple relationships. Teenage couple relationships should be subject to the same adult interest and concern as youthful friendships, other relationships and experiences that are intrinsic parts of growing up and shaping adult life.

In her book, *Teenage Couples: Coping with Reality,*

author Jeanne Warren Lindsay never treats her adolescent
readers or the young people she interviews and quotes with
anything less than full respect. Unlike many books written
for pregnant and parenting adolescents, this book is written
for both young men and women. The words of young men
and women speaking about their lives will win the attention
of teenagers that adult speeches do not.

Teenage Couples is written about teenagers for teenagers, but addresses the teenagers as adults. The life decisions these teenage couples have made have rendered them
adults. As Lindsay writes, "If you're married, or have a
baby, or you're living with your partner, you have pretty
much decided you're through with childhood."

As all good teachers know, the first step to adulthood is
being treated like an adult. Adolescent readers of *Teenage
Couples* will develop an understanding and respect for the
demands and responsibilities of relationships and parenthood through the words of their grown-up peers.

Susan N. Wilson, Executive Coordinator
New Jersey Network for Family Life Education

ACKNOWLEDGMENTS

Many, many teenagers have helped with this book. More than 3,700 completed the Marriage Expectations Survey which is mentioned in several chapters. Results of this survey provided valuable information concerning today's teens' thinking on the topics of marriage and living together. The survey was administered by nearly 100 teachers across the United States, and I appreciate their willingness to participate.

Most of all, I appreciate the teenagers I interviewed in depth. All of these young people had lived or were living with a partner at the time of the interview. Without their insight, their willingness to share their problems, their frustrations, their joys, and their techniques for building a strong relationship, this book would not have been written.

To protect the anonymity of the interviewees, their names have been changed in the quotes, but many of them gave me permission to list their real names here. They include Anna Plum, Lester Bravo, Aimee King, Alyssa Levocz, Amy Bustria, Ashley Harrison, Brandi Rubio, Cheryl Crump, Christi and Chris Coen, Kristine Sharits, Christine and

Raymond Teachey, Christy Boynton, Cynthia Alvarez, Delia
Arellano, Diana Arroyo, Donnell Gaines, Doreen and Rudy
Rodriguez, Emelina Rosario, Erin and Mark Braaten, Priscilla
Correa, Gabriel Garcia, Gabby Barcena, Gwen Godinez,
Isabel and Aaron Goss, Jacqueline and Augusta Dawson,
Jamie Baker, Jennifer Platz, Jennifer Rader, Jerome Sheridan,
Nikki Hill, Joy and Louis Dixon, Kelly Marsh, Leticia
Mendez, Lisa Stoops, Lora Stantz, Mandy Johnson, Jesse
James, Maria Tongko, Mayra Raygoza, Michelle Pack,
Michelle Rico, Travell Dupard, Michelle and Fred Oberst,
Niki and Adrian Ghafoor, Niki Roschewski, Wayne Allen
Saul, Jr., Rosie Vargas, Carlos Villa, Ruth and Isaac Guiza,
Michelle Guilliatt, Marisol and Armando Barrozo, Tino and
Donna Delgadillo, Tisha Brown, Jason Beard, Tammy
Stratman, Wendy and John Monroe, Yvette Ireland, Julio
Gutierrez, and Monica Quintero.

David Crawford's photos add a great deal to these books.
Several people read the manuscripts and made helpful
suggestions. These included Sol Gordon, Sally McCullough,
Eugenie Wheeler, Judy and David Peterson, Trish
Schlichting, Pati Lindsay, Erin Lindsay, Peggy Soule, and
Lois Gatchell. I especially appreciated comments from
Jennifer Oakes, 17.

I thank Joy Dryfoos and Susan Wilson for taking time
from their busy lives to write the lovely Forewords for the
Teenage Couples books. I admire and like them both.

Tim Rinker designed the covers, and Steve Lindsay
oversaw the general design of the books. Carole Blum and
Karen Blake helped with proof-reading and the many other
tasks involved in the research and production of both books.

I especially thank Bob, my love, for his constant support
throughout the researching, interviewing, and writing the
Teenage Couples books, and especially for the forever
relationship we have developed over the years.

Jeanne Lindsay

To the young people
who share so generously on these pages
their struggles and their joys
as they work toward a forever relationship.

*You can expect lots of changes if you marry or move in together.
Is your relationship strong enough to handle them?*

CHAPTER 1

Coping
with Reality

*Our relationship is pretty good, but not like I
expected. You look at all these soap operas, and it's
all nice and everything. They don't deal with a lot of
problems. It's that responsibility thing—you have to
do things you wouldn't normally do. I guess I was
lazy when I was with my parents. My mom did everything for us girls, and now I have to do it all
for myself.*

Carman, 16/Caesar, 21 (Sergio, 2 years)

*You need to sit down and talk about all the respon-
sibility of moving in together—the bills, having money
for food, spending money. You probably won't have as
much as you do now. What will that do to your
relationship?*

You need to talk about everything. Who is going to

help with the chores? Know as much as you can about
what it will be like—before you move in.
    We didn't. All we did was talk about how fun it
would be to have our own apartment. That's about all
we ever said. Getting the apartment was harder than
we expected. Even teens who don't have kids say, "I'm
going to move out when I'm 18. That will be so much
fun." It's a lot of responsibility more than anything.
Angelica, 18/Ricardo, 18 (Jacari, 3 years)

"Coping with reality" sounds a little grim, as if reality is
something terrible to be faced with great difficulty. Adults
may accuse you of having no idea what it will really be like
when you talk about getting married or living with your
partner or having a baby.

They are probably right. None of us can know in ad-
vance exactly what our future realities are going to be. Who
knows what next week will bring, let alone next year? Or
ten years from now?

This is true. It's also true that saying, "Oh, it will all
work out" doesn't make good sense unless you are commit-
ted to doing everything in your power to make your life go
well. We can't know what the future holds for us, but we
can do a lot to shape that future. That's what this book
is about.

Looking at Your Reality

If you're married, or have a baby, or you're living with
your partner, you apparently have decided you're through
with childhood. You're ready to get on with your life.

You're facing a different kind of reality than that faced
by most teenagers. You have a partnership with another
person, a person who needs to be considered as you make
personal decisions, a person, in fact, who needs to be a part
of most of your decisions and planning. You may have

a child, a child who gives you both a whole new set of realities.

When you get married, you sacrifice a lot, but it's worth it. It's harder for us because I didn't have to worry about money before we got married. Now we both realize it takes two to earn the money.

We're having a real hard time right now, but I figure it's not something to give up on. Each of us lost a lot of friends when we got married. We're the only two among our friends that grew up. They still do a lot of running around. We have some new friends, and we get along fine by ourselves.

We've learned a lot. I didn't know anything about marriage and kids, and our parents didn't teach us anything. We just learned it all on our own. We talk more now than screaming and yelling.

Candi, 20/Jeremiah, 21 (Jakela, 2; Kamika, 1)

In *Teenage Couples—Caring, Commitment and Change,* we talked about the emotional part of a relationship. We discussed communication, arguments, romance, sex, jealousy, drug and alcohol problems, partner abuse, and divorce. The theme of that book is building your relationship with your partner through caring, commitment, and change.

You and your partner may communicate perfectly. Perhaps you know how to handle arguments and other problems well. You may be experts at keeping romance alive and having fun together.

Even if you deal with all these challenges successfully, you still have to handle such mundane things as money, living with in-laws, preparing meals, and eating together. It's these day-to-day responsibilities that sometimes become so heavy that love is lost somewhere in the struggle.

If you can't pay your bills, it's harder to have fun together. Even if you enjoy taking walks and other free recreation, your disposition is likely to be affected by money and other day-to-day worries. And so is your partner's.

Your life together is likely to go more smoothly and you and your partner will probably be happier if you plan ahead for these realities of life.

Discussing the Issues

When you're considering marriage or living with a partner, ask yourself and your partner a lot of questions first. For example:

- Where will you live?
- What expenses will you have?
- Who will pay the bills?
- Who will do the cooking?
- What about clean-up?
- How much privacy will you have?
- How will you get to school and/or job?
- Do you want children? How many? When?
- If you have a baby, who will take care of him?
- How much time will you and your partner have together if you're both working and/or going to school?

Your list could go on and on, and each question is a topic you and your partner will want to discuss thoroughly before you decide to marry or live together.

If you haven't yet moved in with your partner, look at the changes you can expect should you do so. Discuss them thoroughly. Is your relationship strong enough to work through these changes?

Most people dream of getting out of their parents'
house to be free—but I wasn't free. I'd always
thought of moving out and doing whatever I wanted,

but now I have another person I should talk to about
my decisions. It was pretty hard to adjust.
> Shanna, 18/Randy, 21 (Larissa, 15 months; Myndee, 1 week)

Importance of Extended Family

Even if you and your partner move out on your own,
both your families will probably continue to be an
important part of your lives.

Two crucial questions to ask yourself are: "Do I like my
partner's parents?" and "Does my partner like mine?" You
aren't marrying your in-laws, but they're an important part
of your partner's life—which makes them an important part
of *your* life. Your relationship with your in-laws can
strongly affect your marriage. If you can start your life
together with the approval of all your parents, your relationship will have a better chance of succeeding.

If you don't like your partner's parents or you think they
don't like you, what can you do to improve the situation? If
you're living with them, it's even more important that you
get along well. Talking through your concerns with them
might be a good start.

If you don't live with them, do you see them often? Do
you try to be friendly? Young people sometimes say, "I
don't like my in-laws so I don't talk to them. I stay out of
their way." This is not a good way to improve the situation.
If you think your partner's family is unfriendly, you need to
try even harder to create a good relationship with them.

It was hard when I first moved in. His mother let
me live there because I was his girlfriend. But
Jeremiah wasn't ready to settle down, and she took
his part. It seemed to me she'd rather he'd be with
somebody else.

When this happens, you keep pushing and keep
pushing. She can't always push you away. I tried to

show her I could get along with her even if she
couldn't get along with me.

At first I stooped to her level. Then I decided we
had to get along for Jeremiah's sake. We can't keep
pulling him in two directions. We get along now. We
have to. I have her grandchildren and my husband is
her son. When the mother and wife compete, it makes
a problem.

Candi

Life Changes, Even at Home

For some young couples, living with one or the other's
parents appears to mean life goes on as before. Mom and
dad pay the bills, cook the meals, and take care of the
home. Perhaps the moving-in partner won't be all that
different from simply adding another teenager to the
household.

It's tempting to assume that you two will simply live
together and your parents will continue to take care of you.
However, if you and your partner are smart, you won't
accept this arrangement. You won't accept an understanding that says life hasn't changed much. It may appear that
way at first. Your relationship and your love can't continue
to grow as you want it to, however, if your parents are still
taking care of you.

I moved in with him and his parents when I was 14.
I was pregnant, and it didn't work. His mother was a
real bitch. She was constantly in our business, con-
trolling, still trying to tell him what to do, trying to
tell me what to do.

After the baby was born, she wanted to be the
mommy. It was not a healthy relationship. We had all
sorts of fights which put a strain on Justin's and my
relationship.

Megan, 18/Justin, 21 (Jesse, 2 1/2 years)

Everyone wins when you and your partner's family like each other.

Being taken care of usually means less independence than most teenagers want. The frequent struggles between teenagers and their parents are, in many cases, an important part of growing up and away from the dependence of childhood. For many teenagers, it's normal and healthy to rebel, in a sense, to break away emotionally from mom and dad.

Often, this is a sometime thing. At times teens rebel; other times, they feel close to their families. For some, it's a time of swinging back and forth between the dependence of childhood and the independence of adulthood.

When it's your partner's parents against whom you'd like to rebel, however, things get more complicated. See the next chapter for guidelines on living with your in-laws.

Preparing for Your Own Place

Actually, living with parents for a few months can give you a chance to prepare for truly being on your own. You may be paying rent to your parents. If you aren't, is either or both of you working? If you have any money, you'd be wise to act as if you're paying rent.

If you put the money in a savings account, you'll be able to have your own place much sooner. The reality that keeps many young couples out of their own apartment is that first and last month's rent, clean-up fee, security deposit, utility turn-on fees, and all the other extra expenses of moving in.

If you continue living with your parents or your partner's, you may not be responsible for many bills. You may do fine financially *if:*

- Both of you are working or one of you makes enough money to support both of you.
- You agree on how you spend your money.
- You don't have a baby to support.

Even as you meet these guidelines, you probably want to plan and save your money so you can get your own place.

If you don't have your own apartment already, take the time to look at available housing in your area. Learn how much rent you'll probably have to pay. Ask about the moving-in expenses. Does the rent cover utilities? If not, how much will electricity, heat, and water cost? You'll need to figure your year-around costs because utilities, especially heat, may cost a lot more in the winter. What about phone expense?

For our budget, we take how much we will have at the end of one month, figure out what our diapers will cost, household supplies, etc. We have our own washer and dryer now, which cuts down on laundry expenses. We pay all our bills first. Normally we put money in the bank, but lately we haven't been able to. We have to do at least one fun thing a month, go swimming or rent a movie.

We pretty much know what our bills will be from the month before. So we set up that budget and try to get enough money at least to pay our bills and have fun with what's left. If we have $40 left over at the

*end of the month, we'll talk about it. It's not that if
there's $20 left over, it's mine.*

Randy

Money Needs Change

A young person "surviving" on a skimpy allowance
from parents might think marriage would mean more
money. If that person's future spouse is earning a regular
paycheck, it's probably quite a lot more than the allowance
from mom and dad.

However, most of the young people I interviewed expressed shock and concern about their financial situation.
They hadn't expected so many bills. If they made the rent
payment, they couldn't afford the refrigerator they needed.
Each time they saved a little money, it had to be spent for
unexpected doctor bills or other emergencies.

Erin Kathleen, 18, and Joe, 21, were married two years
ago. Both talked about money problems:

*Advice? I'd tell people to wait at least until they're
out of high school to get married, and save at least
five weeks pay for back-up money, like loaner money
to you. A lot of money problems happen. People get
married, and there are a lot of money problems.*

If neither of you has a job, don't get married.

Erin Kathleen

*I didn't make a whole lot of money when we first
got married. Before, it was barely enough for me, and
I don't need much. I would have bread and lunchmeat
for sandwiches and I'd have pop in the refrigerator.*

*Lately it's been getting hard. When you make more
money when you're married, you need more things.
Now it's the car payment, rent, and all kinds of stuff.
We have to spend it when the paycheck comes in, or
our bills aren't paid. We're in a pretty big hole now.*

Joe

Money may not buy happiness, but the lack of it causes a lot of unhappiness. Over and over young couples talked about money problems. Living with a partner often changes one's money situation a lot. If you move into your own place, you'll have the rent, the utilities, food, all the bills that your parents handled when you were living at home.

> *Now we're living alone. I always knew it would be hard, because that's how relationships are. They have their ups and downs. There's a lot of responsibility, especially thinking about bills. When we want to go somewhere, we can't because we have to put that $20 into the gas bill.*
>
> Tameka, 17/Zaid, 22 (Chantilly, 6 months)

As you look at your expenses as a couple, stick to the partnership concept. Each of you is responsible for making your lives as a couple go well. If one of you is dependent on the other, your partnership is not likely to work as well over time.

For more discussion of the financial challenges you and your partner are likely to face, see chapters 5 and 6.

Other Realities of Living

The rest of the chapters—food preparation, home-keeping, education and job training, pregnancy, parent-hood—provide useful information whether you're still living with parents or other relatives or friends, or are living on your own.

Are you and your partner discussing who will do the cleaning, the cooking, the yard work, and other tasks of keeping a home going? Before you start living together, you need to understand what each expects of the other. When you don't agree on these important topics, you need to work through your disagreements and come to an understanding with which each of you can live. See chapter 3.

Eating is an important part of life—who will cook? Who will clean up? What if you don't like the same foods? How do you shop for food without spending too much? These topics are discussed in chapter 4.

If either of you hasn't finished high school, doing so needs to have high priority. If you've graduated from high school, you probably need to continue your education and job training. See chapter 7.

Pregnancy changes a couple's life a great deal. Life changes even more after the baby comes. Somebody must be with the baby. Somebody must work. Chapters 8 and 9 focus on these topics, and chapter 10, family planning.

In chapter 11, you will hear from a couple who have been together for ten years, and have successfully faced many of the challenges discussed here and in the other *Teenage Couples* book.

Importance of Self-Confidence

The other book in this series, *Teenage Couples—Caring, Commitment and Change,* offers guidelines for developing a loving, caring relationship. The importance of each person being a self-confident individual who is with the other because s/he *wants to be* is stressed. Ideally, you and your partner are not together because either of you is overly dependent on the other.

This book carries the same message—if you are or plan to be part of a couple, you want it to be a fulfilling, satisfying togetherness. This book, however, provides help with the day-to-day realities—the realities that exist even as you work on your communication skills, continue to keep the romance alive in your relationship, and care deeply about your mate.

Coping well with the realities of your life together can give you a strong foundation for the forever relationship so many of us hope to have.

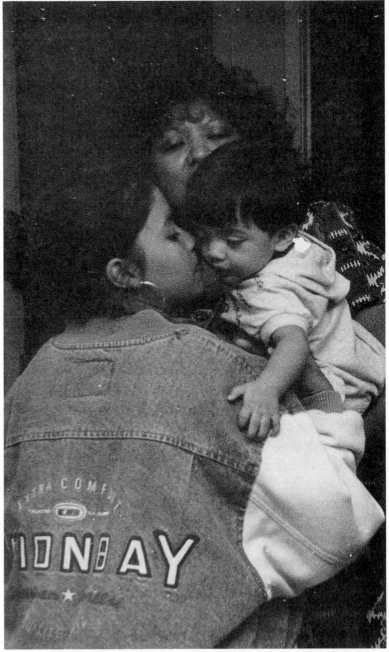

Many young couples live with his parents or hers for awhile.

CHAPTER 2

Living with Your In-Laws

Living with her parents—it's all right, but it's not your house. You can't say, "Let's make a party outside." We stay in this room. It's not the same as having your own place where you can decide things.

Vincent, 20/Karina, 16 (Saulo, 7 months)

When I moved into his house I felt embarrassed to go in the kitchen to get something to eat. They'd think, "Oh, she's eating our food." I felt embarrassed to go to the bathroom. They'd be in the living room watching TV most of the time so I'd stay in my room.

Arlene, 14/Alfonso, 16 (Sylvia, 4 months)

Many young couples can't afford to rent an apartment by themselves. An overwhelming majority of teenage couples live with someone else, usually his parents or hers. Yet slightly more than half of the teens in the Marriage Expectations Survey said they would "rather" or "absolutely" *not* live with his parents or hers.

Many of the young couples we interviewed who live with his or her parents are not happy with the situation. At this point, they don't feel they have a choice.

Set Up Guidelines First

If you're living with your parents, you should help them out. Don't just lounge around the house and do nothing. Buy the groceries. Help with the housework.

If you feel your parents are getting into your relationship, talk to them. Open the communication.

Remember that you're living in their household.

Traci, 16/Wesley, 20 (Elias, 20 months)

Living with in-laws is likely to be difficult, especially if the young couple feel their parents are still treating them like children. The parents may, of course, feel they're acting like children, and resent their apparent lack of responsibility. They figure if the young couple is old enough to live together, they're old enough to do their share of the work and pay their share of the bills. That share may be more for a "grown-up" son or daughter—even if that son or daughter is only 16. Mother and dad may have thought their days of taking care of their kids were almost over—and find instead that an extra one has moved in.

Setting up some guidelines before the partner moves in is important. Everyone involved—his parents, her parents, and the young couple—need to be very open about what each wants, what is possible, and how to work out the necessary compromises. It won't be easy!

Parents, whether they are yours or your partner's, appreciate it if their adult children take on adult responsibilities. And if you're living with your partner, no matter what your age, you're already playing an adult role. Sometimes the responsibilities that go with that role are hard to handle.

What About the Housework?

I was used to keeping house one way. When I came here to live with his parents, they had a whole different set of rules. It was hard for me to adjust.

When I lived with my dad, he didn't care. We tried to keep a clean house, but it didn't really matter. Here we keep a clean house. It took a lot of getting used to.

Tiffany, 18/Shaun, 19 (Keosha, 11 months)

Families vary drastically in the way they keep house. For some people, home is where you relax and spend as little time as possible cleaning up the place. Clutter may be everywhere, but not be a big problem to members of the family.

Another family may feel neatness is most important. Maybe they can't relax in a messy house. Everyone living there is expected to keep everything in its proper place.

Problems arise when family members clash on degree of neatness they want.

Either practice can work, as long as family members agree. It's important, of course, to keep one's home clean enough for health and safety, but the importance of having everything in its exact place at all times varies from family to family.

Problems arise when family members clash on degree of neatness they want. Mothers traditionally nag teen sons and daughters about their messy rooms. That happens, and families cope.

When an extra teenager moves in, however, s/he is

generally expected to conform to the standards of the host
home. Of course it was hard for Tiffany to adjust to "a
whole new set of rules." She was wise to learn those rules
and abide by them.

Housekeeping standards are a good thing to discuss
before one marries or moves in with a partner. Knowing the
rules ahead of time can help the incoming partner adjust to
different ways of living.

> *I don't get involved in anything like shopping or
> cooking at his mom's. Over here with my mom, I was
> in on everything. I cleaned, I cooked, I did everything.
> Over there, I'd ask her where the cleaning stuff was,
> and say I'd help her, but she doesn't want me to.*
>
> *Like once I started cleaning the windows, and she
> told me, "No, that's not how you clean them. I do it
> like this."*
>
> *Normally I'd start arguing, but I bit my tongue and
> said, "Okay, how do you do it?"*
>
> Myra, 17/Sam, 18

Getting the inevitable housework done is a problem in
many one-family homes. Put two families together, and it
can be a real hassle—another problem mentioned by most
of these young people.

Working Through the Problems

> *Judson can't do much because he's gone a lot, and
> my mom gets very upset. When I try to bring it up to
> him, he says, "What do you expect me to do when I'm
> never home?"*
>
> *Mom wants to know why Judson can't do some-
> thing in the morning. In the morning I take the baby
> to daycare and Judson won't get up. He comes home
> at 10 or 11, then sits up watching TV until 1 or 2.
> Then he's too tired to get up.*

*He actually helps less than he did at first. In the
beginning he used to help me out. He used to wash
clothes, not just his. Now he washes his own clothes
and leaves the others. Or I'll leave bottles in the sink
at night because I'm real tired, thinking he can wash
them. He doesn't, and my mom is upset because she
wants everything put away at night.*

Aracely, 18/Judson, 27 (Chianti, 18 months)

Working out a kind of contract may help here. Aracely,
Judson, and her parents could make a rough list of the
things that must be done. How can each person help make
their lives go more smoothly? Perhaps if Judson sees the
list and feels the others are truly doing their share and need
his help, he may be more cooperative.

Or, when the list is made, they may decide that Judson is
doing more than they realize. After all, he works long
hours, he washes his own clothes. Perhaps he should not be
expected to clean up the sink when he comes home. Can
they compromise? Could Judson get up two or three morn-
ings each week and take some responsibility for their
home? It's worth a try.

Erin Kathleen and Joe moved in with Joe's parents for a
short time after they married. Erin Kathleen, only 16,
discovered that she and her mother-in-law washed dishes
differently:

*Joe's mom knew how she wanted things done, and
I had different preferences. Such as dishes. I'd do
dishes, and she wanted them hand dried and I would
let them drain dry. She didn't say anything to me or to
Joe, but she'd get on the phone and talk to other
relatives. She'd say, "I had to do all the dishes over
because she didn't dry them. There are spots all
over them."*

Those first two weeks were real hard because I
didn't know what she wanted. She'd go tell somebody
else instead of me. She helps out, but she wants
people to know all the troubles she goes through. It
made me feel real bad.

                                              Erin Kathleen, 18/Joe, 21

Erin Kathleen was willing to change the way she did the
dishes and other housekeeping tasks. It would have been
easier if she and her mother-in-law could have discussed
these things immediately.

It takes a lot of effort to make a relationship work successfully. It usually takes even more effort to create and
keep a good relationship with parents-in-law, especially if
you're living with them. But if you love your partner, the
extra effort you spend developing a good relationship with
those parents will be worth it.

Not Enough Privacy

Over and over these young couples mentioned the lack
of privacy. They could never be by themselves. Most of
them had one room they could call their own—and they
spent as much time as possible in there. Sometimes they
didn't even have that:

His parents' house had two bedrooms. Nine of us
slept there. In the first house, we slept in one of the
bedrooms. The two small kids slept with their mom,
and one family slept in the living room. Then we
moved, and we slept in the living room. I was on
bedrest for three months of my pregnancy, but there
was no bed to rest on.

I almost had Satira when I was six months along
because it was so stressful. All those months I was
living with them, sometimes I'd go to his aunt's house
because I couldn't stand it.

                                    Stephanie, 18/Kent, 20 (Satira, 8 months)

Sometimes there's not much privacy.

One young woman I visited showed me some shelves in a closet just for her things. Her partner had many brothers and sisters and the house was small. But his parents had made sure she had a little space that was entirely hers. She appreciated that.

Spending time in a park and finding other places to be alone together may help.

When a young couple starts living together, they need time to adjust to each other. If they can live by themselves, they may find they more or less shut out the rest of the world for awhile. They center on each other. Ideally, this process helps them bond to each other, to become really close to each other. If they can't have privacy, this may not happen as easily.

Getting out of the house may be a partial answer. If the weather is nice enough, take walks together. Spending time in a park and finding other places to be alone together may help. If you already have a baby, it gets more complicated. But babies prefer happy parents, and all but the tiniest baby can handle time outdoors with their parents.

Talking over with your family your need for privacy may help. Enlist your parents' help if younger brothers and sisters are forever walking into your room. But first explain your wishes to the brothers and sisters. They might cooperate more than you think. If not, perhaps you can invest in an inexpensive lock and install it on your bedroom door.

Problems with Mom

Several young men mentioned problems between their partners and their mothers, especially if they all live together:

> *Danielle and me moving in with my mom was a problem. I'd been living with my best friend for more than a year.*
>
> *My mom worked all the time and we didn't see her much. When we did, she and Danielle fought a lot, and I'd be stuck in the middle. I'd be at work and Danielle would call me and say my mom said this. Or we'd all be sitting there, and Danielle would say, "Your mom said . . ." and my mom would say, "Danielle said . . ."*

> Jordan, 23/Danielle, 17

Danielle explained her feelings about the situation:

> *We got along great before I moved in with Jordan and his mom. After that, it was real difficult. We were in a one-bedroom apartment, and we were sleeping in her living room.*

> *Things are different, like you're intruding on her space. We were crowded, and we were living out of a closet. She was upset because whenever she had company, we were always there. She's single, and she couldn't have a date over. Before, Jordan was usually gone—he was out with me. But when I moved in, we were usually there.*
>
> *Once when she had company over, we stayed in her bedroom. Most of the time, we'd be there in the living room. The last month, it was real hard because we'd bought a bed for our apartment and set it up in her living room.*

First of all, Jordan needs to level with his mom and with Danielle. He'll not be their go-between. Perhaps each one of them needs to develop some selective listening skills. Jordan's job is not to carry messages back and forth between his mother and his partner. He might be able to smooth things out between them, however, by providing a little insight into their behavior.

Danielle may be missing her mother, and she may feel very alone. It's often hard for a 17-year-old to express her feelings to her mother-in-law, especially if she already feels uncomfortable in her presence.

Perhaps Jordan's mom expected Danielle to be grown up, to act like an adult, when she moved in. Instead, she sees Danielle "acting like a teenager." She doesn't really want the responsibility of another teenager in her house.

Jordan can help his mom understand that Danielle is trying hard to adjust to her new life, but she needs a little help along the way. The help could be as simple as accepting her as she is—a teenager who has taken on an adult role.

Jordan can also help Danielle understand the pressure his mom feels. Jordan, himself, hadn't lived with her for more than a year. She had thought her days of raising a teenager were over—and here she is with her grown son and his teenage wife living with her in a very crowded apartment. This can be hard on a parent's disposition.

If both Jordan and Danielle take a great deal of the home-keeping responsibility, his mother is likely to be more agreeable. If she's working most of the time, as he says, can they relieve her of cleaning duties? Can they have dinner ready when she gets home? Can they find some place else to be when Jordan's mom has company?

It's the 60/60 method we advocate for couples. If Jordan, Danielle, and Jordan's mom each give a little more than their "fair share" to their living together, things will likely go better.

If You're in the Middle

You, like Jordan, may find yourself in the middle of problems between your partner and your mother or father. Stephanie lived with Kent and his mother for six months. Partly because it was so crowded there, they moved back to her mother's house. She reported the difficulties:

> *Kent was raised differently than I was, and sometimes he says, "God, your mom's a witch."*
>
> *I'm always between them. If my mom gets mad at him, she doesn't tell him. She tells me. That's what we mostly fight about.*
>
> *He's working. That's one of the problems. He works in the same company as my mom, and my aunt is his boss. She lives with us. Anything he does wrong at work, they blame me. When they get frustrated with him at work, they tell me about it. Then we don't get along. Sometimes my mom induces a fight between me and my boyfriend.*

That's a difficult situation. If Stephanie and Kent's relationship is to work well, they can't let their families come between them. Stephanie must make it clear to Kent, her mother and her aunt that, while Stephanie is concerned, her aunt must handle job-related problems at work. She needs to talk to Kent directly and help him improve his work performance. Stephanie can't do it for her.

Living in the same house with his boss and his mother-in-law who also works with him must be very difficult for Kent. Perhaps some tension could be relieved if Kent and Stephanie discussed non-job-related problems with her mother and aunt. Maybe they could develop some kind of contract in which they decide who is responsible for various household tasks. Since Kent is working, a monthly fee is probably expected

Does Kent have any other job choices? If not, his role may be to cope as well as possible in order to save enough money to move out with Stephanie. If he doesn't qualify for a different job now, perhaps he could take job-training classes at night. This might prepare him for a job with less friction between him and his boss.

If you have a similar situation, remember that you can only be responsible for your part in relationships. You can't solve problems between other people. If your partner and your mother don't get along, you all need to realize you can't solve their problems for them. You can only love and support both of them.

Siblings Need Attention, Too

At first we didn't get along with my mom. My little sister was real jealous of Kenny because he got so much of my attention. So I stopped giving all my attention just to Kenny. I started taking my sister places with us so she wouldn't feel left out. We let her

push our baby in a stroller when we went somewhere.
        If Kenny and Susie were fighting, my mom would
have to yell at her. When we worked that out, Mom
didn't have to yell at my sister or at Kenny.

Misty, 18/Kenny, 17 (Damian, 11 months)

Showing extra consideration to brothers and sisters is important when a new person moves into the home. Having a new family member changes brothers' and sisters' lives, too. They may feel left out, as Misty's sister did, or they may be upset at losing some of their living space.

Once again, communication is important. Misty showed her understanding and caring when she started giving her little sister more attention. Doing so reduced stress for the entire family.

Different Backgrounds May Cause Problems

If a couple has widely different family backgrounds, it will take even more care to make the relationship work. If the two families don't speak the same language, it can be especially difficult:

I moved in with Sam five months ago because my
mom wanted me to know how he is. It's weird living
there. He's the only child, and his mother is over-
protective. She's scared that she's losing him to me.
        She speaks only Spanish so I have to work at that.
If I do something, she will correct me. I'll say my
mom does it this way, but she will say, "No, do it
this way."

Myra, 17/Sam, 18

Myra speaks some Spanish and she's learning more. She knows it's important to be able to talk with Sam's mother. Improving her Spanish is an important step for Myra because having a good relationship depends a great deal on good communication. As Myra becomes more comfortable with speaking Spanish, obviously she and her mother-in-law can be more responsive to each other's needs.

If you speak English and your partner's family speaks another language, you may find yourself thinking it's they who should change. The important point is that you can't change someone else. You *can* make an effort to speak their language. In the process, you may find their English is improving, too.

"It's Getting Better"

If your partner's parents don't like you, your relationship with your mate may not go smoothly:

> *We broke up just before Larissa was born, mostly because Shanna's parents didn't want me around. Her dad and I had not been close, but I'd been helping him with his car and we talked. Then when Shanna got pregnant, he turned against me. I could understand why they were upset, but I couldn't see why they wouldn't give me a chance.*
>
> *It's getting a lot better. Shanna's dad comes over and talks to me or I'll go over to his garden. Mostly we talk about cars.*
>
> *Her mom was always willing to talk to me although she didn't seem real friendly all the time. It's getting better. They seem to trust me a lot more than they used to. When they first met me, I didn't have a good reputation.*
>
> Randy, 21/Shanna, 18 (Larissa, 15 months; Myndee, 1 week)

Randy's relationship with Shanna's family has improved, as he says. Shanna considered some of the reasons:

> *He was good with my family but they weren't good with him. I'm the youngest, and when I got pregnant, it was hard for them to adjust to it. And I was always*

*the kid with the best grades. They took their
disappointment out on Randy.*

*Things are getting a lot better. My mom communi-
cates with him, and so does my dad. There isn't
always tension when they're around each other.
Randy never gave up on my parents.*

Shanna

The key here is "Randy never gave up on my parents."
That's an important concept, and a hard one to follow. If
your partner's parents act like they don't like you, it's hard
to keep trying. When you do, you all may win.

How to Move Out?

You may know you want to live by yourselves. If you
have a child, you think he'd be better off if you could move
out—but you don't have the money. Maurice felt this way:

*We're living with my mom and my sister. I want to
move out because we're kind of confined to our room,
and Lana needs her own room. But I can't even
imagine where I would get an extra $350/month more
than we have now. We're getting some things ready
for when we can.*

Maurice and Mitzuko go to garage sales. Already they
have a crib for Lana. There's not much room to store
furniture at Maurice's mother's house, but last week they
found a used sofa for $50. They put it in their bedroom—
which leaves little extra space. They decided it was
important to get started preparing for their own home.

They don't have room for much more furniture, but
they're watching for inexpensive pans and other kitchen
items as they go to garage sales.

Remember the old-fashioned hope chests our great-
grandmothers prepared before they married? Little girls
filled chests with linens and other necessary items in

preparation for their marriage. You're following their good example when you get a head start on furnishing an apartment of your own.

You and your partner, like Maurice, probably want to plan and work toward a place of your own. If either of you hasn't yet finished school, however, be sure you do whatever is necessary to get those diplomas. If that means accepting help from parents, that's what you need to do.

While a place of your own may not be a practical goal today, it's worth sacrificing now to be able to live as you and your partner want to live later on.

Whether a young couple lives with his parents, her parents, other relatives, or friends, they are likely to have a difficult time. Lack of privacy, disagreement over who does the housework, and how to raise the children are just a few of the problems to be expected.

If you and your partner can't afford a place of your own, you need to sit down with your families and talk about the best solution to your where-do-we-live question. Once a decision is made, everyone involved will need to work hard to make things as comfortable as possible for everybody.

In the meantime, if you're living with your partner's parents or yours, you'll be ahead if you trust, respect, and care for your extended family and your partner's. If you do, you'll find your relationship with your partner has a much better chance of succeeding.

For a more thorough discussion of living with your partner's parents, or having your partner move in with you and yours, see *School-Age Parents: The Challenge of Three-Generation Living* (1990: Morning Glory Press).

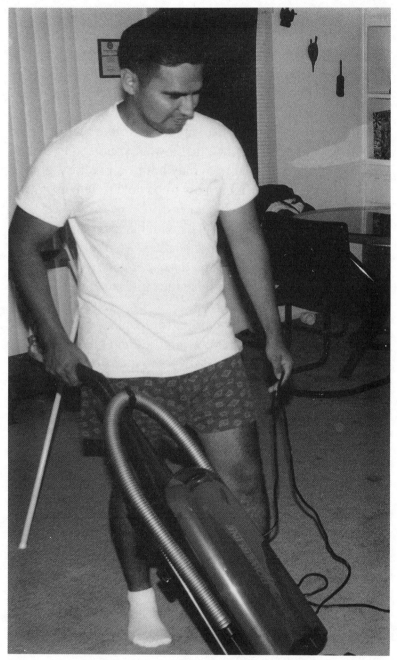

Partners need to share home-keeping tasks.

CHAPTER 3

Sharing the Tasks of Living

I'm quite messy. When I was younger, the women in my family did most of the work. They cleaned up after me. When I made a mess, I didn't have to worry about it. They did it.

Now that I'm married, I can't do that. Selia can't be cleaning up after a grown man, so I'm trying to be more neat with my clothes. Selia told me, "I refuse to be a maid." I knew I had to change.

I'm working and Selia is at home, so she does most of the work while I'm gone.

I like to cook, so I do all the cooking.

Child care is a shift type thing. Most of the time Selia does it. If she gets tired, then it's my turn. Most of the time I get up at night.

Enrique, 19/Selia, 19 (Riquie, 11 months)

*I believe this is a team effort. We both have to
work and do things at home. We both help out with
the housework. I'm the more cleaner person so I work
harder at the cleaning, but that's because of what
I want.*

*I'm pregnant now, and I'd get sick if I had to do
those dishes. Joe does most of the dishes now.*

*I work at night so he cooks dinner for himself.
When I'm home at night, I'll cook. Sometimes I cook
a real meal on the weekends.*

                                        Erin Kathleen, 18/Joe, 21

Living together brings obvious changes to a young
couple's life style. Perhaps you've had your own room all
your life. Now you'll share it with your spouse. And the
cleaning—for some people cleaning takes on added importance after marriage—or becomes more of a hassle.

Teenagers have a reputation for being messy. Parents
have been known to call their son's or daughter's room
"The Pigpen." Young people who delay marriage for
several years after high school often learn how to get along
with other adults through living together in a college dorm
or moving into an apartment with friends. But one who
moves directly from a parent's home into life with a partner
may not realize the importance of compromise in daily
living. One partner may not be as willing to pick up after
the other as mom was:

*I think he'll admit he's a slob. I get frustrated. He
leaves his shoes where he takes them off—and we
have a closet right next to the door where he could
put his shoes. Instead, he walks all the way into the
living room and takes them off and just leaves them
there.*

                                        Erin Kathleen

Some people have lived with a mother who always cleaned up after them. When they get married, they may expect the other partner to do the picking up and the cleaning. Again, talk it through *before* you start living together.

If you know before you marry that both of you are fairly messy, you can do some planning together on coping. Will one of you pick up after the other? Or will you each be responsible for your own mess? Will you take turns? Or. . .?

Who does the dishes in your home? Mows the lawn? Repairs the car? Vacuums the rug? Feeds and diapers the baby? A couple of generations ago, such questions had easy answers. In most homes, the woman took care of the house while the man was in charge of the car and yard.

This was a workable arrangement for many people. The man was expected to get and keep a good enough job to pay the bills. His big responsibility was to support his family.

His wife, then, was supposed to take care of things at home. She cleaned the house, cooked, took care of the children, washed the clothes, and sometimes took care of the yard and garden.

For many families, this arrangement worked well because the wife didn't hold an outside job. Homemaking was her full-time job. Anyone who has kept a house clean, cooked three meals each day, and taken care of small children knows that it is indeed a full-time job.

Roles Are Changing

I clean a lot. Sometimes I cook, but other times I'm too tired to do that. But I pitch in.

My dad didn't. He was lazy—that's why my parents got a divorce.

You have to work as a team.

Troy, 21/Sandra, 18 (Violet, 16 weeks)

Today, the picture has changed in many families. First, most families can no longer get along on one paycheck. Many couples, including those with small children, find they both need outside jobs in order to pay the bills. The wife may work as many hours away from home as her husband does.

Some women are not satisfied doing "only" the housework. Not all women like or are good at cleaning house or cooking. Not all women want the total responsibility of child care. Many prefer to earn part of the family's income.

In some families, the woman is expected to wait on her husband. When a young man from such a family gets married, he may expect the same kind of service from his wife. If she doesn't think this is right, they will need to do a lot of talking and working through the problems that may arise.

Sam and Myra have already worked through some of these differences:

> *Sam already knows I'm not going to be like his mother. His mother washes everything for him and she irons it. If it's not right, he'll yell at her. I tell him, "If I do it for you and you don't like it, you can do it."*
>
> *Sam will tell my mom, "Will you get me a drink?"*
>
> *She says, "You have two arms and two legs. You can do it." He's so used to his mom that when he started going out with me, he wasn't used to the idea, "If you want something to eat, go get it." I'm not going to be like his mother, and he accepts it. My mom says he has changed a lot since we started going out.*
>
> *The first year he'd get mad if we wouldn't get him something like his mom would. Then he started realizing he could get it himself. His parents are real*

old-fashioned. The men never go in the kitchen, and they never cook.

Myra, 17/Sam, 18

Sam talked about the changes in his life since he and Myra have been together:

Of course I'd like a traditional marriage because that's the way I was raised. I'd love it if Myra could stay home and feed me, but I know women today aren't like that.

It's the way my mother is. She has never worked a day in her life, and she waits on us hand and foot, and my dad is in charge. What my dad says, goes, no questions asked. I've never needed anything, and my mom has never been without. That's the way I'd like to have it, but I'm not in Mexico.

Myra is real clear. She's not going to wait on me. Like she says, we're in this together. I can handle it.

Sam

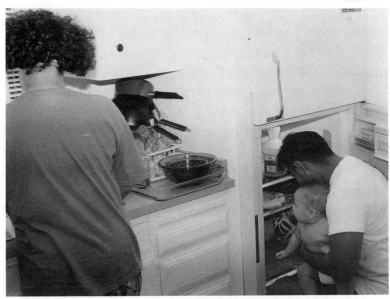

Sharing kitchen tasks is a good partnership-builder.

If the young couple must live with his family when they're first married, it may be especially hard. Even if they talked through these differences before they started living together and came to some agreement, his family may be critical of their equal partnership. Sitting down with his parents and discussing these issues may be helpful.

Two Essentials: Paycheck, Housework

If neither partner wants to hold a paying job, trouble looms ahead. Unless they are independently wealthy, they will have obvious problems with no income. Welfare grants do not provide enough money to live as most people want to live.

Perhaps their parents will help out for awhile, but help from parents is likely to run out at some point. Anyway, most young people cherish their independence. If mom and dad are paying the bills, they're probably also making many of the decisions.

Most of us would agree that someone needs to earn some money. Both partners can't stay home and keep house. Most of us would also agree that someone needs to wash the dishes and sweep the floors.

So what happens if both partners *choose* to hold outside jobs—or find that both *must* work away from home? What if neither one wants or has time to do the housekeeping chores?

One Person, Two Jobs?

Perhaps your father was lucky enough to come home tired after a day's work, and be able to sit down to a hot dinner. After dinner he read or watched TV while your mother cleaned up the kitchen. Your mother may not have had a full-time job away from home. If that was their division of tasks, fine.

That model still exists in some homes in which both
partners work at a full-time job. Or one may be working
while the other attends school full-time. Either way, each
has a full-time job away from home. Yet some husbands
still expect their wives to clean the house, cook the meals,
and take care of the children in addition to working or
going to school full-time. This translates to one person
holding *two* jobs and the other, only one. While this surely
is not a fair or reasonable division of tasks, Vincent, whose
wife attends school full-time, is convinced it's the way
it's supposed to be:

> *I feel the man has to bring in the money and the
> woman has to do the housework.*
>
> *My mother was always home. Sometimes Karina
> tells me, "You think like the old-fashioned people
> think. We're in the 90s."*
>
> *I say, "I don't care if we're in the 90s, I expect you
> to iron my clothes, clean our room, fix my meals." It's
> probably because that's how my mom was.*
>
> *We argue about responsibility that Karina has to
> take as a wife—things that she has to do and she
> knows that she has to do, but she doesn't do them. She
> waits for me to tell her, "You have to do this."*
>
> *Then she says, "I'll do it." But she waits 40
> minutes to do it.*
>
> *We don't talk that much, only when we have argu-
> ments. I explain myself to her, what it is I don't like.*
>
> *Karina was offered a job and she'll have an
> interview soon. It's okay with me if she works. I know
> we'll have a problem with her working and doing all
> the housework because she'll be out of the house a
> lot. I might clean our room, share the housekeeping a
> little.*
>
> Vincent, 20/Karina, 16 (Saulo, 7 months)

Karina talked about her feelings concerning their traditional marriage responsibilities:

About a month ago I had a hard time cooking for Vincent. I'd say, "No!" Lately, I talk to myself in my sleep, "Get up and cook him something before he has to tell you." Vincent never cooks. If he does, it's because we're mad at each other and I don't want to cook for him. But then he's so mad at me for the rest of the day that it's not worth it. It really hurts when he's mad at me.

I make myself get up and iron his clothes. I'd like to be appreciated, but he doesn't say anything about it. I'd like to hear, "Oh, thank you for doing this for me."

Vincent really doesn't have any responsibilities except bringing home the money. I tried working for a month, but I couldn't be a wife, student, mother, and work. Vincent gave me a choice, that either I would quit and be dedicated to this, or stay at work and keep on having fights. I couldn't handle it.

Karina

Vincent and Karina are disagreeing on a very basic issue. Couples who start out as determined as Vincent to keep the strict role-playing of husband earns the money and wife does everything at home don't fit well into our society—*unless* the husband actually earns enough money to support his family in the way he and his wife want *and* she is happy taking care of the house and not working away from home. Vincent and Karina don't seem to be meeting these criteria in their relationship.

If Karina continues to keep house and not have an outside job, she should be able to feel this is at least partly her decision. At this point, Vincent seems to be in charge rather than the two of them having a true partnership.

Two Paychecks Preferred

In the Marriage Expectations Survey, only one-sixth of the males and one-sixteenth of the females thought the husband should be responsible for earning all the money. Almost 70 percent of the males and 90 percent of the females thought the couple should share this responsibility. A few said it was the wife's responsibility.

The majority of respondents also felt partners should share the various home-keeping tasks such as vacuuming the house and mopping the floors.

About two-thirds of the females and almost as many males (60 percent) said both should prepare meals. Almost three-fourths of the females and two-thirds of the males said both should clean up after meals.

Slightly more than half the females and 42 percent of the males thought both should wash the car. Even fewer—38 percent of the females and 31 percent of the males—thought both should mow the lawn. For these jobs, the man was more likely to do the work.

While many women don't want to do all the housework and child care, not all men enjoy yard work or car repair. More important, many men don't want the total responsibility of earning the money for the family. The stress of having a wife and children solely dependent on his paycheck can be very difficult.

A few families do a complete role reversal. She works away from home and he becomes a househusband. If one paycheck is adequate, he takes responsibility for cleaning, cooking, and child care, and both partners prefer this approach, wonderful! They are lucky to agree. However, according to the marriage survey, only one-third of the teenage women responding said it would be all right if her husband wanted to stay home while she got a job to support the family.

Any of these three approaches can work if both partners choose to follow it. Both partners may choose the traditional approach where the husband works and she takes care of their home (assuming he earns enough money to support his family). Or she can work while he keeps house. Or both can work, and both can share housekeeping tasks.

Problem of Housework

If one of you wants to work and one of you wants to stay home, great. You can probably work out a fair and acceptable division of tasks. This works if two things are happening: The person working is earning enough money to support your family. The person staying home is the kind of homemaker you both want.

But what do you do if both of you must or want to work, but neither wants to get involved in the cooking, cleaning, laundry, and other tasks at home? That's the problem faced by many couples today.

If you aren't yet married or living together, talk a lot about how each of you feels about this subject. If you're a girl dating a boy who makes cute remarks about "woman's work," don't ignore it. Ask what he means. Think through together how you would handle lots of different situations. What if he's injured and can't work? Or simply can't make enough money to support your family? What if you get sick and can't cook and clean for awhile? What if you decide you want a job?

If you're a boy dating a girl who suggests that a man will "take care of" her, don't ignore it. Ask what she means. You need to go over the above questions, too.

If either of you thinks one paycheck will be enough, carefully check out your probable expenses, allowing for the unexpected expenses that always occur. Most families must have two paychecks to pay their bills. Talk about sharing the many tasks necessary in running a pleasant home if both of you are working.

If you are a woman and your partner was brought up not to do "woman's work," you need to figure out some re-training techniques. You need to tell him things need to be different.

If you do everything at home and he does nothing, you don't think it's fair. You can't help it if that's the way he was brought up—that's not the way it's going to be.

> *I usually cook, and Shanna cleans the kitchen. I clean the living room, and whoever needs laundry, does it. I do the garbage because she doesn't like to do that.*
>
> *It usually works out pretty good. Sometimes Shanna lets the kitchen lapse, so just to be spiteful, I'll let the living room lapse. It gets to be a big pain, and we have to spend the weekend cleaning.*
>
> *Shanna will leave dirty diapers on the floor, overnight even, plus clothes on the floor. But I make a bigger mess in the kitchen than she makes in the living room. It all balances out pretty much.*
>
> *We got out of the traditional roles through trial and error. When we first got together, Shanna was working and her mom was head honcho at her house.*
>
> *We argued about it. I said, "You should clean the house."*
>
> *She said, "You should clean it."*
>
> *There was no way she could take care of the kid, go to school, clean the house, cook, take out the garbage. And I don't like dirty kitchens.*
>
> *Whatever needs done gets done. I don't know how we broke out of it. I don't think we ever really got into who was dependent and who was not.*
>
> Randy, 21/Shanna, 18 (Larissa, 15 months; Myndee, 1 week)

Shared Roles Work

*My mom always had to do the housekeeping, and I
don't believe in that because I'm working and Joe's
working. If I didn't work and I stayed home, then
maybe I could do the housework. With both of us
working, we need to share it.*

*Joe usually washes the outside of the car and
waxes it because he's afraid I'll scratch it up. He has
me vacuum the inside.*

Erin Kathleen

More and more couples are sharing both roles. Each has
a paying job and each shares in the housework and child
care. Both the man and the woman can benefit. He isn't
burdened with all of the financial responsibilities and she
doesn't have to do everything at home.

Hopefully, she will be able to find a job she will enjoy—
just as he wants to like his job. He may enjoy some of the
household tasks, too. He almost certainly will find he
becomes much closer to his children if he is involved in
their care.

*I feel it's important for the man to do his share of
those things. I grew up where my mother stayed home
and raised the children and my dad did the work.*

*I have a feeling in me to take care of my wife like
he did, but when I see my wife doing all these things,
it's important to help her out. I change the baby a lot.
She's breastfeeding, so I do the changing and hold
Valizette while Davina gets adjusted.*

*We both get up at night. I hear Valizette, and I get
up. Davina may be feeding her, but I'm there to
change her if she needs it. A kid needs her dad
involved.*

Johnny Angel, 19/Davina, 19 (Valizette, 11 days)

Johnny Angel is giving himself a wonderful start in parenting. He's developing the close relationship with his daughter that he'll always treasure.

Disagreements over who does which task at home and who earns the money can ruin a relationship. If you're honest with each other, and each of you remembers the magic of providing lots of trust, respect, and caring for the other, you'll probably be able to work through these dilemmas. Hopefully, you'll find a style of living that satisfies both of you.

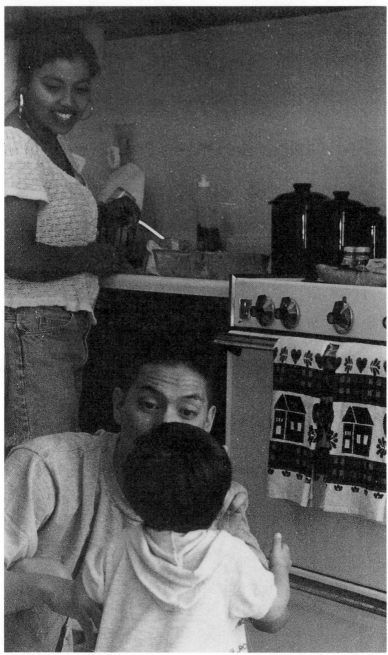

Everybody helps cook.

CHAPTER 4

Three Meals a Day— Forever!

At home I had no real responsibility. I used to help my mom, but not like this. I get tired. I have to wake up at 4 a.m., drive to school, then come home and clean up the house. It's hard, but I have to do it.

I shop for the three of us on Fridays. At first it was hard because I didn't know what to fix. Ishmael goes shopping with me, and at first he'd tell me what to buy, what he likes. Now I know the things he likes. Our food tastes are similar. I look for things we both like.

He cooks more than I do. I like that. I do most of the cleaning.

Lorraine, 16/Ishmael, 19 (Renae, 27 months)

Right up there in importance with where we live is what we eat. You and your partner are lucky if both, or even one of you already knows how to cook. Life goes easier when we have good meals.

Encouragingly, of those in the Marriage Expectations Survey who already live together, about two-thirds of both sexes said his/her partner is a "good" or "excellent" cook.

Who's Going to Cook?

In some families, everybody cooks. In others, mom does most of the meal preparation. Sometimes girls and boys grow up learning to cook by helping mom. Others don't have that experience.

I had never cooked because my mom babied me. When I started, I burned everything. I don't use recipes. I do things I've seen people make. I call my mom or my aunts, and they tell me how to do it.

When Troy gets home, I have the hamburger out, and I have the hamburger helper out. He loves noodles. He likes pizza, and we have frozen pizza for him. Then I have a salad and vegetables. We don't eat much fast food because it costs more.

Sandra, 18/Troy, 21 (Violet, 16 weeks)

Before you marry or move in with a partner, talk about the all-important topic of eating. Who is going to prepare the meals? Who will clean up? In some families, the woman does both. That's fine *if* she has the time and both partners agree this is her job. However, if she has a job away from home and gets home later than her partner, who should cook? They may agree that it's his job, and she will clean up after dinner.

No matter who usually cooks, *both* partners need to be able to fix simple meals. If she's out of town on a business trip, or she's just had a baby, he'll be fixing the meals. If he goes away to visit his family for a few days, she'll be in charge of the cooking.

Learning to Cook

If you aren't married or living with a partner, and
you've never cooked much, consider learning how to
cook simple meals now. This will help when you, with
or without a partner, move out on your own. You'll be
glad you did!

> *If I had stayed with my family, it would have been
> better. My mom would have showed me how to cook. I
> felt dumb asking Caesar's mother. I would watch her
> and see what I could learn.*
>
> *I suggest that everyone learn to cook before they
> move in with someone else. Caesar pressured me a
> little. He didn't want his mother to cook for me. His
> mom told them they had to be patient because I had
> never cooked.*
>
> *I turned the tortillas with a fork because I was real
> scared to cook in front of them. They would always
> laugh at me. I'd laugh with them, but I didn't like it.*
>
> *I tried recipes, but it just didn't come out like
> the picture.*
>
> Carman, 16/Caesar, 21 (Sergio, 2 years)

Recipes don't always come out looking as great as the
picture in the cookbook. The dish may taste good, however.
Recipes can be a big help for people who haven't cooked
much—and for those who like to try new things.

If neither you nor your partner knows how to cook,
taking a cooking class might be a good idea. If you don't
have a learn-to-cook class at your school, check the adult
education catalog for such a class.

If you don't know much about cooking, or if you're busy
with other things, you'll probably look for shortcuts:

> *I hadn't cooked before, and I still don't cook very
> well. We have spaghetti from a jar. My mom is a real*

good cook, and she says I should make my own sauce.

Sometimes I get the ready-made salads. Or I'll cut up tomatoes and cucumbers and buy ready-cooked shrimp and throw it in the salad. We buy frozen pizza and other frozen foods a lot.

Tameka, 17/Zaid, 22 (Chantilly, 6 months)

Fast Foods Often Expensive

We used to eat a lot of fast foods before we moved out by ourselves. That was when we had extra money. Now we get pizza once or twice a month.

Nathan says he's going to turn into a chicken because I fix a lot of chicken. We aren't home to-gether for evening meals, so on Sundays I cook a meal and we all sit down and eat together. Hopefully, we'll have more time this summer when neither of us will be in school.

Katelynn, 17/Nathan, 20 (Daron, 21/2 years)

Nutrition is important for the whole family.

Fast foods are popular with many teens. However, if you're on your own, you may find you can't afford a lot of fast food. If you shop carefully, it's usually cheaper to prepare your meals at home. Nathan explained:

Little things add up. Katelynn wanted to buy pizza every other day. Then she was telling me she didn't have money for her prom dress or her shoes. I told her if she wanted it, she had to get it. So she did it. She worked a little longer each day, and she quit buying pizza.

She realizes now that with all the money she has spent on pizza and clothes, she could have a car.

Nathan

Different Families, Different Foods

He cooks different than I do—like chicken soup. We do it with chili. I fry the chili first, but he doesn't. He said mine was good, but he likes the other way best. Usually I don't fry it now. Actually, it's easier this way.

*I learned about chilies, those big red ones. Another chili—I don't know what it is, but it's **so hot**. We both like it. We both like hot food although he'll add more than I do. If I don't put chilies in the food, he won't eat it.*

Lorraine

Your family may eat foods quite different from those your partner's family likes:

There's a big difference in our food habits. He was raised on real spicy homemade Mexican food. I was raised on the "normal" food—steak and baked potatoes.

His mom had her own grinding stone to make
tortillas. And no matter what you eat, you eat tor-
tillas. I tried, but I couldn't do it every single night.

Meghan, 18/Justin, 21 (Jameka, 2½ years)

Meghan smiled as she said "normal" food. She knows
Justin's spicy food is just as normal as the foods she had as
she grew up.

Summer found a simple way to serve her partner the
spicy food he likes without having to eat hers with the same
seasoning:

Daesun likes spicy foods so I cook mostly spicy for
him. I don't really like spicy things so I cook his
portion last and add more spice.

Summer, 15/Daesun, 20 (Cecelia, 9 months)

Vincent compared his mother's cooking with
Karina's:

My mom used to make me a lot of quesadillas,
enchiladas, other Mexican food. My wife only knows
how to cook eggs, potatoes, chicken, and the kind of
tortillas I don't like. I like flour but she gives me corn.
I have to deal with that. My mother made tortillas
every single day. Karina knows how, but she doesn't
like to make them.

Vincent, 20/Karina, 16 (Saulo, 7 months)

When he adds, after voicing his dislike of Karina's
cooking, "I have to deal with that," he means he has to eat
what she fixes. True—if she's in charge of the cooking. He
could ask his mother for a cooking lesson—for himself. He
could learn to fix quesadillas and enchiladas. Mexican food
could be his specialty. By sharing the cooking, they could
have a more varied diet, and each could serve some of their
favorite foods.

As for corn versus flour tortillas, perhaps they could buy or make flour tortillas half the time, and corn the rest of the time. Compromise works with food preferences, too.

Dealing with Different Tastes

Maurice and Mitzuko each discussed their quite-different food preferences, and how they deal with those differences:

With food, Mitzuko and me are in completely different worlds. Me and my family, we eat meat with every meal. You have to have some kind of meat. She's from a family that could eat a casserole for every meal.

I don't mean to be racist, but she was raised by her white grandparents. For example, she'll eat pumpkin pie and she'll eat sweet potato pie. Her mom is Korean so that gets even more into it. Mitzuko is into Chinese food and Korean food—like marinated cabbage plus she eats rice all the time. It's funny because I grew up on rice at almost every meal and I hate it.

Plus she thinks she wants to be a chef or something so she cooks these meals she reads out of books or learned at school and uses me as a guinea pig. Most of the time, I have to admit, it works out pretty good.

Maurice, 21/Mitzuko, 16 (Lana, 14 months)

Mitzuko's food tastes, as Maurice says, are quite different from his family's. Mitzuko lives with them, but she decided she could be in charge of meals for herself and Maurice most of the time. She commented:

I cook except on Mondays and Tuesdays. If I don't cook, somebody will cook something nasty I don't like.

They don't eat three meals a day. They just eat
when they want to. So I try to make a meal about 4
or 5 o'clock before anybody else cooks something.

His mother fries too much stuff. She loves pork
chops that are fried, and fried chicken. That's not
good for you. I don't like so much grease. She made
meatballs with gravy and rice once, and it was nasty.

I follow a lot of things we do in our teen parent
class. Every Thursday we cook in class. Last week we
learned to make chili, so now I make chili. I learned
the shortcut—you just buy beans in a can.

Over spring break I'd make dinner one day, and
the next day we'd have the left-overs for lunch. That's
the way I grew up, you eat left-overs for lunch.

Not only may a couple have different food preferences.
They may vary a great deal in how fast they eat. If you're
used to eating quickly and your partner is an extremely
slow eater, you will have some adjusting to do. To enjoy
your meals together, one of you may need to relax more
while the other speeds up a bit. Again, compromise is
important in relationship building.

Thinking Ahead

I've had to learn to organize. Be sure you thaw the
food in the morning. If you're living with your in-
laws, try to have your own refrigerator. I have a
separate little part of the refrigerator, but the kids get
into it. There are six kids under 15, and I'd like to
have a refrigerator in our room. I keep everything
that won't rot right here.

Karina

There are several things to think about when you're
planning meals. Of course you choose foods you and your

partner like and can afford. Unless you want to spend lots of time cooking, you look for easy menus. Breakfast can be as simple as cold cereal, milk and juice. Or you may prefer to fix a bigger meal.

If you eat lunch together, this, too, will probably be an easy meal. Peanut butter sandwiches are a standby for many people, whatever their age. Macaroni and cheese can be cooked in less than 15 minutes. Another quick dish most people enjoy is refried beans (canned if you prefer) and grated cheese on a tortilla. Top with salsa if you like. Just fold the tortilla over and heat in the oven or microwave. Add milk, carrot sticks and fruit and you have a well-balanced meal.

As you plan meals, aim for good nutrition—you and your partner need to stay healthy. Good food helps you have more fun because you feel better. You'll probably also have fewer doctor bills if you eat well because you'll be healthier. Emery Dean understood this, to April's surprise:

He always makes sure we have breakfast. He's like one of those nutrition freaks, and he makes sure we have a good dinner, too. It's kind of weird. I have never seen a guy do that before.

My mother and I take turns cooking. If it's something I've never done, she shows me.

April, 18/Emery Dean, 19 (Patrick, 22 months)

Nutrition for Good Health

The Food Pyramid (page 71) is a good guide. Most people get plenty of food from the protein group. All you need are three servings of meat, cheese, refried or baked beans, or other protein food. Have a little protein at each meal and you'll have plenty.

Maurice's family ate a lot of meat. I'm not a big meat eater plus meat is expensive. I buy some

*hamburger meat. I usually plan the food I'm going to
fix—probably hamburgers one night, hamburger
helper one night, some stir-fry meat because I love to
make stir-fry.*

Mitzuko

If you are a vegetarian, you can get plenty of protein
from cheese, dried beans, and other non-meat protein
foods.

Do you like milk? It's a marvelous food, and, as a
teenager, you need three or four glasses each day. If you
can't drink milk, cheese and yogurt will also provide lots of
calcium for you and your family.

Most people like fruit. You and your partner need two to
four servings each day. If you have orange juice for breakfast plus a banana on your cereal, eat an apple as a snack,
and have fruit with lunch and/or dinner, you'll have plenty.

Vegetables are a bigger challenge for some people. If
you don't much like cooked vegetables, do raw veggies
taste better to you? Raw vegetables, of course, are not
limited to carrot sticks and radishes. Other veggies that
taste good raw include cauliflower, broccoli, mushrooms,
green and red pepper, cabbage, lettuce, jicama—and you'll
find others at the supermarket. Experiment to find those
you and your partner especially like. Veggies and a dip
(refried bean dip, for example) make a great snack.

On the bottom row, the foundation for the Food Pyramid, are the breads, cereals, and pastas. Most people like
these foods, and for good health, need to eat six to ten
servings each day.

Notice the tiniest part of the Food Pyramid contains fats
and sugars. That's because we need very little of these
foods. Holly talked about the reasons:

*I grew up in a house where we couldn't eat salt or
fat because of my mom. I don't go to the extreme of*

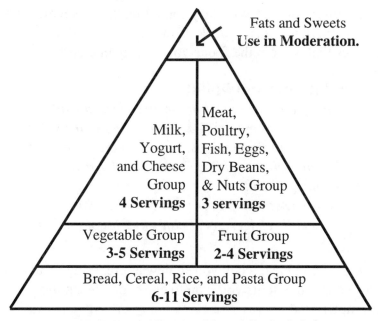

Food Guide Pyramid — A guide to daily food choices

eating chicken every night, but I watch the
cholesterol.

   Curtis doesn't care. Recently he had his choles-
terol checked, and it was the level of a 65-year-old
man. So we cut back. We're eating healthier, better
than we were. We eat chicken now when we go out.

Holly, 18/Curtis, 28

Look at the Food Pyramid as you plan your meals. For
many families, breakfast and lunch are much the same day
after day. Dinner, however, is often the meal for which you
spend a little more time and effort.

If you don't know how to cook a lot of different things,
find a basic cookbook—or a cookbook with "Simple" in its
title. *Yo! Let's Eat!!* by Pat Adams and Marc Jacobs (1994:
National Resource Center for Youth Services) is a cookbook written especially for teens. You might like it.

Promise yourself you'll try something new every once in awhile, perhaps once a week. If money is limited, choose recipes that contain the foods you usually buy anyway.

Planning Your Shopping

I like planning meals two or three days ahead because it saves me time. Otherwise I go to the store and look at all those things. Then I go crazy because I don't know what he'd like to eat. I think I save money by planning ahead.

I still have to shop every day or two because we have a small refrigerator. I can't fit a lot of food in.

Carman

It's a good idea, when you're new at preparing meals, to write down the items you plan to cook for a week. For example:

Monday: Tacos, watermelon, milk
Tuesday: Hamburgers, salad, French fries, milk
Wednesday: Chow mein, rice, fruit, milk
Thursday: Pizza, salad, milk
Friday: Hamburger Helper, green beans, cole slaw, milk

Make a list before you go shopping. Shop when you aren't hungry—you'll buy more if you're starving!

I shop twice a month. Usually I get everything the first time, then the second time, it's perishable things like milk and eggs. I generally plan what I'm going to make before I do my shopping list.

If you go once, you get what's on your list and that's it. If you keep running to the store every day, you spend more money. "I think I need this. I think I need that," and it just sits there in the cupboard. I figured that out, plus I took a nutrition class in the GRADS program. They had a nutrition expert talk to us about shopping and cooking.

*Best thing is coupons—I have a coupon for
everything.*

Katelynn

Mitzuko and Maurice, like many of us, don't have a lot
of money. They tried three different ways to go shopping.
They don't have a car. Surprisingly, they discovered they
could actually save money by calling a cab after a well-
planned shopping trip. This way, they could shop less often, and buy more things than they could carry on the bus:

*I'm trying to budget my money so I can have
things.*
*At first we tried to wait to go shopping until we got
a ride there and back. But that would take a while, so
we started taking the bus. We'd just get food we could
carry home. Then we found out that if you go shopping more often, you spend more money. So now we
get our money together for the food, go there on the
bus, buy all the food we need, and then we call a cab.*

Mitzuko

Eating is an important part of our lives. Respecting each
other's food likes and dislikes helps a couple's relationship
thrive. Eating the right foods makes us feel and look better.
Planning meals can help us fix more nutritious food and
possibly save money and time.

• Sharing the cooking works best for many couples.

• Cooking class and recipe books can help.

Good cooking and good eating!

Too many bills cause frustration and worry.

CHAPTER 5

Dollars
Make a Difference

We moved in together two years ago. Since then, every penny we have goes for the bills and for the kids. Basically that's it.

I'm working the same place five years now. If I didn't work, I don't know where I'd get money. I can't depend on my parents—and I'd rather do it on my own.

Jeremiah, 21/Candi, 20 (Jakela, 2; Kamika, 1)

It's just hard, worrying about bills, making sure the rent and the heat are paid. A lot of times I don't want to think about those. I'd rather be buying a new outfit. When I was with my mom, I didn't have to worry about it.

Tameka, 17/Zaid, 22 (Chantilly, 6 months)

I've worked since I was 14. I have two jobs now,
and I'm in college.

The hardest time was when we moved into our own
place. We had to get a deposit and the first month's
rent. We moved in the middle of the month so we had
to pay rent again in two weeks.

I used to be real bad with money because when I
lived at home, I didn't worry about anything except
clothes and gas. Now I have money in the bank. I save
my money, pay the bills when they come, and spend
what's left. I just work, go to school, and pay bills.

We handle it by setting priorities. If you want to
buy new clothes and you have rent due, you'd better
pay the rent first. Those new clothes won't keep you
warm if you're stuck outside.

Nathan, 20/Katelynn, 17 (Daron, 2 1/2 years)

Most of the young people we interviewed for this book
spoke of money problems. Many who were living together
and/or married said money—or the lack of it—has been a
greater problem than they expected.

Sharing Spending Responsibility

Sandra wants a lot of things. I tell her we can't get
those things. We've got important things to do with the
money, bills, saving up. Sometimes we get into it, and
she gets mad if I don't give her money. I do, but
sometimes there isn't enough left after the bills.

Troy, 21/Sandra, 18 (Violet, 16 weeks)

Some teenagers are skillful at getting money from their
parents. It's a game they play. If this game continues into
marriage, it's not good at all. A couple needs to put *our*
needs, not *my* needs and *your* needs, at the top of their list.
A couple's basic survival needs have to take priority.

Ideally, neither partner plays parent. They look at their bills and other necessary expenses together. They decide together how to spend the money they have. This is hard to accept for some teens who are used to parents providing them with more spending money than the couple can now afford.

It's hard for me to give Danielle everything she's used to. She is very spoiled, used to having her own way. If she got in a fight with her parents, they would buy her things. They didn't know how to handle a teenager.

We have very different ideas on spending. We can go in a store for one thing, and she will want all these other things. She will say, "I really, really want this."

And I will say, "If we had the money, we'd do it." I'm getting $321 a week. If we can get our bills caught up, our budget will work.

Jordan, 23/Danielle, 17

Danielle explained her feelings on their money problems:

Mostly we argue about money. He's 23, so a lot of times it seems like he's acting like my father, trying to boss me around. I think a marriage should be 50-50. Nobody should control the other one.

I like to get things like the other girls at school. They don't understand that I can't because we have to pay the phone bill. I like to go out to the movies, but we don't have the money, and it bothers me.

Danielle

Of course it's hard not to be able to buy the things one's friends buy. But Danielle needs to realize she is no longer her parents' little girl. She's right in thinking marriage should be 50-50 and that "Nobody should control the other one." To do that, she and Jordan need to work together to make their money cover their expenses.

Soon after the above conversation, Danielle reported their plans for managing their money together:

A lot of times I've said, "Forget it," and I go out and get what I want. Then we couldn't pay the bills. So now he'll pay the bills and I'll keep the records. Hopefully it will work out. I'm going to start working a lot more, too.

Each week when he brings home his check, we'll decide what it has to go for, and we'll make sure we each have $10 for the week. Whatever we have left is what we can spend. This month has been especially hard. We have taxes due, and I have a lot more bills this month.

Sometimes it's the woman who is the better shopper:

We don't agree on spending the money. He goes to the supermarket and picks everything. He won't look at things and compare. He just spends money. I look for the cheap one that's just as good. We argue about that.

The other day he bought the baby a bib that cost $4. I didn't get mad, but I told him, "You're very dumb for doing that because we could have gotten two for that price."

Janita, 16/Elijah, 19

Telling Elijah he's "very dumb" isn't a good choice of words even though he paid more than necessary for the bib. Perhaps he and Janita could shop together and look for good buys. Wise shopping takes experience, something Elijah apparently needs. Perhaps Janita can help him get it.

"I Earned It. I'll Spend It."

Sometimes a man feels that if he works while his wife "merely" keeps house and looks after the children, the money he earns is his to spend as he pleases. He doesn't think his wife should be involved in deciding how to spend it. Joni, who was 15 when she married Jeff, 18, had this problem at first:

We always argue about money. Jeff thinks because he makes the money, he has more right to use it. So I say, "No, I clean the house, I take care of Angela. I'm doing a job, too. Just because you work for the money doesn't mean you earn it just for yourself." He says it's our money, but he has more right to it.

Most of our money goes for payments, and some- times when there is a little extra left, I ask, "Can I have a little money?" Jeff never wants to give me any. I guess he doesn't trust me. Maybe when I get out of high school I'll get a job so I can have some spending money.

When I want to go somewhere I have to ask Jeff for money. Last week I went to the Amusement Park with my friends, and he gave me $5. Everybody else had to pay for most of my rides. Even his sister told him he should give me some money each week. But he won't.

Jeff didn't understand why this mattered to Joni:

We do everything together so I just pay for what- ever we're doing. If she goes out with her friends, I give her money.

Several months later Joni and I talked again. She and Jeff had had some serious discussions concerning her need for some money of her own. Until Joni finishes high school, getting a job away from home doesn't seem like a good idea. They came up with another plan, however, which involved some changes in their spending plan:

He's including me in the financial part now. I clean his mom's house once a week, and he says, "Now you know how it feels to work and have your money all gone." Which is true. We work hard, and then the money is gone for rent, utilities, food.

His mom made us about five envelopes—one for rent, one for food, another for car expenses, one for utilities, and one with just a little money for me. It's not much, but now I don't have to ask Jeff for every cent I need.

We get our check, get it cashed, and we put so much in each envelope. We've tried this before, and it works pretty good if we stick to it.

Joni and Jeff are beginning to develop some valuable money management strategies. Most important, they're doing their financial planning together now. Their system of budget envelopes is a good way of handling fixed expenses before spending money on impulse purchases.

Handling a Checking Account

Do you know how to write checks and balance a checking account? These skills are important when you start housekeeping and paying your own bills.

Money is one thing we should have talked about. When we got married, I didn't know anything about checking accounts, paying bills, whatever.

When we first opened our checking account, we really messed it up. I didn't even know you were supposed to balance your checking account. Derek had no idea either.

We'd get these statements and I'd just throw them away. Then three months later our rent check bounced. I couldn't understand it because I knew my math was right. But I hadn't deducted the $4 check charge.

When the check bounced, Derek didn't blame it on me although he did think we were both being a little stupid. So we went to the bank, and they explained it all to us.

Gloria, 18/Derek, 18

If you don't know how to balance a checkbook, find out! You can pay bills with money orders instead of checks if you prefer.

I know how to manage money. I waited a long time to open a checking account because I was afraid we'd write checks whether we had the money or not. I balanced my checkbook from the beginning.

I only buy the things I need. I learned from my mom, when you go shopping, you go with coupons, and you look for sales.

Melissa, 17/Jeff, 20

What About Credit Cards?

Jarrod spends his money on beer, and that makes me real, real mad. Then I like to get my nails done, and he doesn't see how I can spend money like that.

Jarrod wants a credit card, and I don't want him to get one. I think it would put us in the hole forever. That would mean we'd have to pay bills, and we don't need more bills to pay when we're trying to get ahead. If he has money in his pocket, he will spend it. If he had a credit card in his pocket, he'd use it.

Anita, 18/Jarrod, 25 (Jarrod, Jr., 4 months)

With a credit card, you may buy more than you can afford.

Many people talk as if they pay for everything with the "plastic"—their credit cards. This may be convenient, but it can easily lead to overspending.

Now when I have money I try not to spend it on things I don't need. Scott is going crazy with me. He doesn't have money, and he's putting everything on charge. I don't think it's right. It's nice of him to buy me a rocking chair and a heater, but I didn't ask for it. He put it on charge, and I don't know how he's going to pay for it.

Celina, 17/Scott, 20 (Melanie, 6 weeks)

Buying things with a credit card, then not being able to pay the bill on time is not the way to get things you want. Before you use a credit card, know the extra charges you will have. How much interest will you pay on your monthly balance? You pay less when you pay cash.

---

*If you choose not to buy on credit,
you're smarter than most of us.*

It is wise, however, to earn a good credit rating. If an emergency comes up and you have no money, buying on credit may be necessary. If you have never charged anything, you haven't built up a credit rating. With no credit rating, most stores won't let you buy on credit.

So it's a good idea to charge something you *know* you can afford. Make your payments promptly. This is how you earn a good credit rating. If you choose not to buy anything else on credit, you're smarter than most of us.

Cutting Baby Expense

Most couples find their money problems get worse when they have a child. First, if you don't have good medical insurance, the expense of having a normal delivery is amazingly high. If a Caesarean delivery is required or other complications develop, costs zoom much higher.

If the baby is bottle-fed, you'll find that formula is quite expensive. Economy is one reason you may want to consider breastfeeding. In chapter 11, Donna and Tino point out that, because Donna is breastfeeding their baby, they are saving nearly $1,000 this year, money they would have spent on formula if she weren't breastfeeding.

The other major immediate expense is a supply of diapers. Many young parents are using disposable diapers for about the same reasons that most of us prefer Kleenex

over a cloth handkerchief. They do save some work.
They're a wonderful luxury.

That's what they are—a luxury. If you can afford disposable diapers, great. But realize what you're doing. Just
because "everybody" uses them doesn't mean you have to,
too. Take the time to figure the cost per year in using cloth
diapers versus diaper service versus disposable diapers.
When you're figuring the cost of using cloth diapers, know
that you will need about four dozen, and include the cost of
laundering them in your cost comparison.

You may be told by a diaper service salesperson that
their service is actually cheaper than buying and washing
your own diapers. Ads for disposables will suggest they are
cheaper. But if you read the fine print—or ask the salesperson some questions—you'll find they're counting the
market value of your time in their comparison.

They include the detergent and laundromat expense in
washing diapers. In addition, they count the amount you
would be paid if you were working at a good job during the
hours you spend washing, drying, and folding diapers. For
most of us, that's not a valid comparison.

Diapers can be folded while you watch TV. You
wouldn't be earning money doing something else if you
weren't folding diapers. So it really doesn't make sense to
include that in your cost comparison. If you do your
comparative shopping carefully, you'll find that disposable
diapers cost at least $300 *more* per year than buying cloth
diapers and washing them yourself. Cost of the diaper
service lies somewhere in between. The difference can be
even more if you buy the highly advertised and most
expensive brands of disposable diapers.

Another possible problem in using disposable diapers —
if money is short, will you be able to buy enough diapers to
change baby as often as needed? It might be tempting to

"economize" by not changing her often enough. An uncomfortable baby, and possibly a painful diaper rash, might result.

Or toilet teaching may be started too soon in order to save money on diapers. That's not a good reason to start putting baby on the potty. Her readiness is the important criteria for this task.

> *Caesar and I argue a lot about the diapers. He thinks Sergio should get off his diaper. I don't think he's ready.*
>
> *Caesar asks, "Why do you change him so much?" I don't change him so much—he just needs to be changed.*
>
> Carman, 16/Caesar, 21 (Sergio, 2)

You and your partner may decide there are other luxuries on which you'd rather spend that $300. Your baby won't care. In fact, some babies are allergic to disposable diapers. Because the more expensive brands are more likely to be highly perfumed, it's these brands that tend to cause allergies in some babies.

Another reason not to use disposable diapers is the environmental issue. Our landfills are reaching their capacity, and disposable diapers are part of the problem.

How Much Baby Food?

You can also avoid spending a lot of money on little jars of baby food. We know now that it's best to wait at least four to six months after birth before giving a baby any solid food at all. Most babies do best on formula or breast milk alone during this time.

By nine or ten months, your baby probably will be eating chopped and mashed (but non-seasoned) food from your table. Instead of buying strained food for those few months between, you may prefer to make your own. You can do so very easily either with a blender or a babyfood grinder. The latter can be bought for very little money.

Many parents spend money on elaborate toys for their baby. Before you do that, check a good child care book for suggestions. Many of the toys on the market aren't especially effective as playthings for an infant or toddler. You can find better "toys" in your kitchen cupboard.

Katelynn offered more tips on buying baby things economically:

> *You can find a lot of stuff at garage sales. When I first had Daron, I had nothing except a crib. A neighbor sold me her baby's stroller and a bunch of baby clothes for $50. Sometimes I find brand new things at garage sales. Resale shops are good, too.*
>
> Katelynn, 17/Nathan, 20 (Daron, 2½ years)

Saving Money with Coupons

Several teenagers I interviewed talked about saving money by using coupons at the supermarket. Janita explained how:

> *I learned to shop with my mom. She compares brands, which one is cheaper and will do as well. She taught me how to clip the coupons. Last time we saved almost $30 with the coupons. Elijah wasn't like that before, but I got him into it. He likes the idea now, so he helps save coupons.*
>
> *We always shop together, and he's getting used to using coupons. He thinks the cheap brand won't be as good, but he's learning. We look at price per ounce— we get more for this one for less money, and it tastes good. So he's learning to look at the quantity and cost.*

*To save coupons, you can go to the Dollar Store
and get a little coupon book for less than $5. Then
buy the Sunday newspaper because it has a lot of
coupons in it. Clip the coupons—canned foods, baby
foods, snacks, breakfast foods, etc.*

*Before I started organizing them, I would find
extra coupons I forgot to use when I got to the regis-
ter. Organizing the coupons is the most important
thing because you'll find you use them all instead of
just a couple. Almost everything I put in the cart has a
coupon for it.*

*We shop monthly, so I save coupons for a whole
month. I collect my coupons every Sunday. I sit there
for hours clipping coupons. Elijah is really getting a
kick out of it now, while before he couldn't stand it. It
gets to be kind of a game.*

Janita

One caution about using coupons—Don't use coupons
to buy things you don't need and wouldn't buy if you
didn't have a coupon. *If you need the item*, coupons can
help your money go further.

As your relationship develops, you will find that wise
spending of the money you have can prevent problems
between you and your partner. Managing your money
together is the best way to go. If one of you has more
experience or more skills in money management, that
person may take the lead, but work this out together.
You'll both be ahead.

Writing down your expenses is a good way to work toward a budget.

CHAPTER 6

Less Stress
With a Budget

We buy our own food and we pay rent on time. We try real hard so we can get used to it. I want us to get prepared for the time we can have our own place. We've been on a budget, so much for food, gas, clothing.

We try not to waste a lot of money. Vincent likes to spend money, but I make sure he doesn't. I tell him, "Think of the baby. He needs diapers." I get $10 allowance every two weeks.

We decide together where the money goes, although mostly I do because he likes to spend it. We'll get about $2,000 from the IRS. He says he needs it for his car, but I remind him the baby needs a new car seat.

I'm proud of us because we don't waste our money

*on things like clothes and stuff. I know someone who
is married and has a baby girl. They spend a lot of
their money on clothes for her, for him, for their
daughter. They have very nice clothes. They're
renting a room, and they don't have a car. I look at
her clothes and I like them—but we have a car. We
don't have to depend on someone else for
transportation.*

Karina, 16/Vincent, 20 (Saulo, 7 months)

*I figured how much money we make together, and
I figured how much we could save each month.*

*You think you can save so much money, but it
doesn't work out that way. You think you can save all
this money—on a piece of paper it looks okay, but it
doesn't work. There are some things we really need
that we didn't plan. And then we have unexpected
doctor bills.*

Erin Kathleen, 18/Joe, 21

When a Budget Is Necessary

Most people aren't interested in working out a budget
until they have money problems. A lot of us go along
spending as we want or need to, figuring it will all work
out. If the bills generally get paid, we aren't interested in
thinking about a spending plan. Not until we see that it isn't
working out—that our bills seem overwhelming—are we
ready to think about budgets.

One day I was talking with a group of pregnant teenagers about the expenses of raising a child. One young
woman said, "I just spend the money until it's gone, and
then I don't have any for the last week of the month. I'd
rather do that instead of budgeting. That would take all the
fun out of it."

But when she was asked if it mattered if there was no food for the baby during that last week of the month, she said, "Of course. That's different." She wasn't ready to talk about budgeting right then, but she probably will develop an interest in the subject sometime after she has her baby.

Myra's mother is helping Myra and Sam plan ahead for the expenses they'll have after their baby is born:

> *My mom takes Sam to the store and shows him how much things cost. He can't believe the prices. We bought soap to wash the baby's clothes and it cost $6. My mom says it's rough out there, and it is.*
>
> *Sam and I argued about money once when he wanted new rims and new tires for his car. I said, "No, you should save the money for the baby."*
>
> *He said, "No, I'll tell my dad to buy them for me."*
>
> *I said, "What's so important about the car?"*
>
> *Sam said, "But the baby isn't here yet." So he asked his father—and his father didn't get them for him. That's when we talked, and I said he really needs to grow up and be thinking about what's coming. He can't just be thinking about his car when the baby is here.*

Myra, 17/Sam, 18

Myra understands how expensive babies are. She knows that she and Sam are going to have to plan their spending very carefully in order to be able to buy the things their baby will need.

Keep Track of Expenses

If you've decided you need to cut back on expenses, where do you start? You may have some areas where you know you're overspending. Or you may be thinking, "We can't cut back. We buy only what we really need."

*We're going through changes with the money. We
didn't really realize the importance of budgeting our
money. When we get it, we spend it.*

*Right now we're trying to buckle down and budget.
We put some in the bank and don't touch it. We pay
the bills, and then what's left over is for leisure
activities. If we don't have any left, we'll have to wait
until next time.*

Enrique, 19/Selia, 19 (Riquie, 11 months)

Whatever your situation, the place to start is *not* to sit
down at once and write out a firm spending plan in which
you cut everything in half. You wouldn't follow it. You'd
get upset. Some of your expenses can't be changed without
a drastic change in your life style, a change you don't want
and may not need to make.

Instead, start your "Let's spend less money" project by
keeping track of *everything* you spend for at least one
week, preferably for a month. You already know what
you'll spend for rent. How much are your monthly utility
bills? Do you have a car payment? Keep track in detail of
car expenses. Don't forget the insurance payment even if
it's not paid every month.

What other monthly bills do you have? Do you pledge a
certain amount to your church? Are you paying monthly
doctor bills or health insurance? Do you have installment
payments to make?

Add all of these payments up. Your total tells you the
specific bills you must pay each month.

*When we started paying our own bills, I put down
on paper what we needed for the baby, phone, everything. I still put down what I have to pay, and take
that from my check. My mom is a bank manager, so
she has always taught us to keep our money managed*

and to never fall behind. We all know about the
checkbooks, what we're supposed to do each month.
Anita, 18/Jarrod, 25 (Jarrod, Jr., 4 months)

Now comes the hard part. Write down every cent you spend—and ask your partner to do the same. Both of you may feel this kind of record keeping takes the joy out of spending. But remember, this is a very short-term project.

How much of your money goes for convenience foods such as TV dinners?

Each time you eat out, keep track of the amount you spend. Each time you buy a coke or a beer, do the same thing. Perhaps more important, keep track of what you're spending at the supermarket. How much of your money goes for convenience foods such as TV dinners? Does either of you pick up a lot of expensive snacks which add very little to the nutritive value of your meals?

What about clothes? Does one of you feel the other spends a lot on clothes? Keeping track of the amount will at least clarify the issue.

What are you spending for recreation? Often, we think it's our partner who overspends, not ourselves.

If you have a child, how much do you spend on him? Parents often feel their child is "worth" whatever they spend. Of course he's "worth" it—but who are you really splurging for when you buy that expensive toy? Your toddler would probably prefer to play with something from your kitchen.

How much are you spending for baby food? Disposable diapers? Keep track.

I have a friend who was talking today about how
they don't have much money. She says every check

she gets she spends on the baby—clothes, etc. I was
thinking, "Your baby doesn't need new clothes every
time you get a check." The baby doesn't care.

A lot of Lana's clothes were given to her. I have a
friend whose baby is a year older than Lana. The
clothes are recycled.

Maurice has always bought lunch at work. But
now we're starting to make his lunches, and that
will save.

Mitzuko, 16/Maurice, 20 (Lana, 14 months)

Be sure you both realize, however, that this brief attempt
at writing down everything each of you spends is simply an
information-gathering experience. At this point, it must not
be a value-judgment issue. If you have thought for a long
time that your partner overspends on food items, don't grab
that first day's spending record as a chance to say, "I told
you so." Keep track, but don't try to change or reach any
conclusions right now.

Cutting the Costs of Living

Are there any surprises in your spending records? Where
do you see extras you could manage to do without? Only
you and your partner can answer that question. But knowing exactly where your money goes is an important part
of budgeting.

Food, for example. You're lucky if the two of you agree
most of the time. When you consider that you each grew up
in a different family with different food habits and different
food preferences, it's amazing you agree at all.

Whether or not you agree, no one else can tell you where
you should cut back on expenses. For some people, buying
a higher grade of meat is important enough to cut out snack
foods. Someone else may realize they can get enough
protein from cheaper cuts of meat or from other protein-

rich foods. To cut out snacks would take away an important area of pleasure in their lives.

Budgeting is a way to get more fun out of your money.

The same kind of thinking applies to convenience foods such as TV dinners and other already-prepared foods. From a strict dollars and cents standpoint, convenience foods generally offer you less food, certainly less nutrition, for your money than do foods made from scratch. You're not likely to get as much nutrition or satisfaction from a TV dinner as from a freshly cooked meal—and the TV dinner usually costs more.

This is not true of all convenience foods. If you bake a cake, you'd probably spend more on the ingredients to make it all yourself than you would pay for a cake mix. Frozen orange juice is usually cheaper than squeezing oranges yourself.

If both of you are working full-time and you can afford them, convenience foods may be an important part of your home management plan. All I'm suggesting is that you and your partner analyze *your* life style. Then decide how to spend your money so that you two get as much satisfaction as possible from the money you have.

Making a Budget

Too often people think talking about a budget is talking about ways to be miserable while saving one's money. However, budgeting really is a way to get *more* fun out of your money.

To work out a budget, choose a time when neither of you is overtired. It's not wise to work on a budget when either of you is already feeling crabby.

*Don't forget a small slush fund or allowance
for each of you.*

With your spending record in front of you, work out
some simple categories. Food, shelter, transportation, baby
needs, recreation, medical, and insurance are some starters.
What did you spend for each? Does one look a little heavy?
Talk about it—and even more important, perhaps—*listen* to
what your partner is saying. A budget works only as well as
the people involved are willing to work at making it work.
Try hard to budget something each week for savings.

> *I've been doing research on budgets. We should
> have at least five weeks pay saved in the bank for
> unexpected things. We should always replace it when
> we spend it—keep it there at all times.*
>
> *That's what I'd do if I could go back to before I
> got married. I'd have at least five weeks pay saved in
> the bank so we'd have money to fall back on. We've
> had a lot of money problems, and we're trying to save
> for a down payment for a mobile home.*
>
> Erin Kathleen

One very important comment: Don't forget a small slush
fund or allowance for each of you. It shouldn't be big
because your money will stretch further if you plan together how to spend most of it. But a small amount per
week should be budgeted for each of you to spend *with no
need to account for that spending.* A few people seem to
enjoy keeping track of every cent they spend, but most of
us don't. Having a few dollars that are mine, that I don't
need to discuss with you, can take a little of the pressure off
our money situation.

A shopping list can save you money when you buy groceries. You aren't as likely to buy things you don't need if you have a list with you. See Chapters 3 and 5 for more tips on food shopping.

Of course it doesn't matter whether the man or the woman takes the lead in handling your money. You may agree this will be the one who has had some experience in money management and finds time to take care of it.

A big advantage in following a budget is that this so often cuts down on one's impulse buying. Do you know you need to spend this much for rent, that much for food, and more for transportation? If so, it may be easier to say no to the person who rings your doorbell, then tells you about his wonderful photo offer, carpet cleaning plan, encyclopedia "special," or other schemes designed to help you spend your money.

Incidentally, it's always best not to make a hasty decision to buy something from a salesperson at your door. Learning to say "No" is an important part of budgeting. If it's something you need, you'll almost always get a better price through comparative shopping in the stores.

Spending Plan Should Suit You Both

If your money doesn't last from one payday to the next, you have two ways to work at solving the problem. You can try to figure out how to earn more money, or you can cut back on your spending. Neither method is easy. For most of us, neither method is much fun.

We both had to get used to not having money. As long as we have food and a roof over our heads, we're okay.

I think now that we're both working, things will get easier. I didn't want to work—I'm real picky about who keeps the kids. But I found somebody I can trust

and that's good with them. That was a hard decision.
When I'm at work, I still worry—but I know she's
good to them.

Candi, 20/Jeremiah, 21 (Jakela, 2; Kamika, 1)

You may be thinking that some day when you have more
money, you won't need to do all this budgeting. Certainly
having "enough" money to be able to make decisions on
how to spend it is a lot better than not having enough to pay
your bills. But most people still have money problems even
as their income increases. Careful planning makes that
income go further, however.

Money is a problem with everybody. It seems like it
doesn't matter how much I make, or whether we're
both working, we have the same amount—none.

I was roofing and making a lot of money for
awhile, but it didn't make much difference. We just
bought a few more things.

Randy, 21/Shanna, 18 (Larissa, 15 months; Myndee, 1 week)

It's important not to spend more money than you have.
It's often wise not to charge a lot of things. It's important to
have an emergency fund waiting for that unexpected illness
or when your car breaks down.

We kind of let bills slide for awhile at Christmas so
we could give the kids a good Christmas. We set our
priorities—we normally don't let bills slide. We plan
it out. We try to set up a little budget and keep things
rolling. But we always have unplanned expenses, like
running out of diapers three days early, two days
before payday.

Shanna's parents are understanding and help us if
we need it, but I don't like doing that. I guess it's the
guy thing.

Randy

Present or Future Oriented?

Some people live for the present—and others for the future. Present-oriented people see no reason to save for the emergency that isn't here yet. They prefer to enjoy today rather than sink all their money into a house at some future date.

> *Angela is more a short-term person. We have money right now so why not spend it? I'm more long-term—we need money for the last week of the month. I try to plan, but she sort of messes up my plans.*
>
> Juan, 18/Angela, 16 (Vaneza, 7 months)

Future-oriented people are willing to make sacrifices now in order to have a more secure future. Saving for emergencies, planning how to buy a home later are important goals for them.

There are as many different ways to handle money as there are people handling that money. For couples, it's probably most important that they find together a style of money management that fits *them*.

If they feel more secure scrimping and saving for that rainy day, that's what they should do. If, on the other hand, both prefer to live more dangerously, they may get away with it. If they don't agree, they need to communicate their different viewpoints to each other. Then they need to find compromises with which both can cope.

To manage money well, the most important thing is for you and your partner to be happy with the way you're managing the money you have. Be sure, however, that *both* of you are involved. It's the agreeing on money matters that's important to your entire relationship with each other.

That first job is an important step toward your future career.

CHAPTER 7

The Challenge of Finding a Job

I was in school when Angela moved in. Then when she got pregnant, I went looking for a job. I wouldn't really call it a burden, but it was hard. I'm only 18, and it took me awhile to adjust. It happened real quick.

Juan, 18/Angela, 16 (Vaneza, 7 months)

*There's nothing in this world, not even the baby, that will guarantee he'll be with me the rest of my life. My mother wants to divorce my father but she has no job, and she has six kids. That's why she puts up with him. I **have** to finish school.*

Karina, 16/Vincent, 20 (Saulo, 7 months)

Marlene's pregnancy was a surprise. You have to grow up overnight. I was scared. I was a senior in high school, and I didn't know how I was going to deal with it, or my folks, or the rest of my family.

*I was going to go to college this year, but this set
me back a year. I wasn't working yet when Marlene
got pregnant. Then I started going to school for just
half-days, then working in the afternoon for a building contractor. I did that until about August, and then
I went to work as a TA* (teacher's aide). *I really enjoy
this work, and I plan to major in education.*

Jeremy, 19/Marlene, 16 (Amber Marie, 7 months)

Do You Have a Job?

If you're living together and you're under 20, you
probably don't have as much money as you'd like—unless
your parents are wealthy and very generous. Time after
time, the young people I interviewed talked about money
problems, especially when they moved away from their
parents' home into a place of their own. Continuing your
education and getting job skills is even more important for
you if you live with a partner—and a really big deal if
you're already a parent.

Joe and Erin Kathleen were married two years ago when
she was a sophomore in high school. Joe had graduated a
few months earlier. When asked about money, he replied:

*Money? What money? It goes quickly. I've got a
lot of friends that didn't get married, and they have
all this stuff. When you're married, you don't have
that much money. I chose Erin Kathleen over all that.*

*I started working right out of high school. At first,
I'd miss days if I didn't feel too well, or I'd leave
early, come in late. But when I got married, I went
every day, sick or well, it didn't matter. When you get
married, you have a big responsibility. I need all the
money I can get.*

Joe, 21/Erin Kathleen, 18

Erin Kathleen also had a job when she and Joe were married:

I started working in a nursing home doing dishes when I was 14. Now I work in a medical clinic as a nurse's aide. I help with X-rays and other procedures, and I love doing it. I want to be an RN (registered nurse), and I'm starting my training this fall.

Erin Kathleen

Erin Kathleen and Joe are expecting their first baby in a few months. They're working hard so they'll be able to support their baby as well as themselves.

Importance of Education

Ricardo feels bad because he's not a good reader. I tell him to get into a learning center and they'll help him. He says they would laugh at him.

He wanted to get married, but I said we can't until he gets a good job. I know that if someone doesn't want to get into school, he won't. Now he says he's going back, and I hope he does. When he's ready, I'll be there to say, "I'll help you if you need help."

Angelica, 18/Ricardo, 18 (Jacari, 3 years)

If you or your partner hasn't completed high school, that's surely your first goal. If either of you has dropped out of school, now is the time to return.

For awhile, when we'd get to school, Brad would say, "Let's leave." My attendance went down because I wanted to be with him. When I realized I was going to have a baby, I knew if I didn't have an education, I wouldn't have anything. I didn't want to work at McDonald's all my life.

Jessica, 15/Brad, 15 (Rodney, 4 months)

Jessica and Brad are no longer together, and Jessica is working hard to continue her education:

I'm trying hard to finish high school. I'm in a program now for four hours a day at the YWCA, but I can stay only one semester.

There is no program for parents at the high school. We've tried to talk to the school—there are so many girls with babies. I think the school expects the girls with babies to drop out, but we want to be somebody like the others do. I want to finish my education, but they aren't helping me at all.

My grandparents are going to try to help me with child care, and I'm trying to work out something with the neighbors. It's hard to support the baby.

I'm on WIC (Women, Infant and Children food program), *and they give me the formula. I'm working. I don't have welfare. I work 30-50 hours a week. When I go back to school, I'll continue working.*

Eventually I'd like to go into law or some kind of law enforcement. Or I'd like to be a paramedic. I like helping people.

                                                                    Jessica

Finding Child Care

Not having child care at school is often the cause of young parents dropping out of school:

I had to stop school in December because I didn't have a baby-sitter. Friday was graduation, and I felt real bad that I wasn't part of it.

Kenny is a year behind me. He said, "Well, go back next year, and I'll try to graduate with you." They're going to start a daycare center here this summer. Then I can go back.

                              Misty, 18/Kenny, 17 (Damian, 11 months)

If your school doesn't provide day care for students' children, can you and the baby's other parent go to school or work at different times so one of you will always be with the baby? Is there anyone at home or in your extended family who will take care of your child while you go to school? What about your neighbors?

If none of these ideas are possible, talk to other young parents. Can you take classes at different times, and take turns taking care of the children? If you're getting welfare, ask your social worker about programs designed to help young parents become job-ready. There may be some help there.

Help with Education

If you are married and your spouse is in the Armed Forces, check on the education benefits to which you're entitled. April's husband is in the Navy, and she plans to take advantage of Navy spousal benefits:

> *I want to be a paralegal or a pharmacist tech. Next spring I want to go to state college, mostly at night time. Then I won't have to worry about day care because Emery Dean will work in the day and take care of Patrick at night. The military pays for 75 percent of my education.*
>
> April, 18/Emery Dean, 19 (Patrick, 22 months)

If you're both in high school, you may need help from your parents. If you have a child, you may qualify for AFDC (Aid for Families with Dependent Children) while you finish school.

If you need financial help to finish high school, you'll be ahead if you accept that help. Most people don't like to accept welfare. Even if you qualify for this kind of aid, you won't get enough to live as you'd like to live. But if that's

what it takes for you to get an education so you can be
independent later on, the sacrifice will be worthwhile.

> *In this society, that college degree is going to help*
> *me get a good job. I know people without degrees*
> *getting $5 an hour and friends doing the same thing*
> *with a degree getting $9-$10. You have got to go to*
> *school. If you don't think so, look at the baby.*
>
> Elijah, 19/Janita, 16 (pregnant)

Is Welfare Enough?

Only 12 percent of the young people in the living-
together survey reported they were depending on
welfare for support.

For most people, AFDC doesn't provide the support
they need. The amount available to a single parent varies
widely from state to state. Sue receives welfare for
herself and her child, but she finds it doesn't go far:

> *I get $70 a month to spend on Jonathan including*
> *diapers. It goes pretty fast.*
>
> *I also get $62 each month for going to school*
> *through a special program. If I miss more than four*
> *days a month at school, I'll lose that. So far I've*
> *managed, but I don't know what I'll do if Jonathan*
> *gets sick.*
>
> *I'm in a GRADS program. That helps me learn*
> *about babies. We both want to work so we won't have*
> *to worry about money. We're really struggling now.*
>
> Sue, 17/Rick, 20 (Jonathan, 7 months)

GRADS is the name of school programs for school-age
parents in Ohio and in some other states. If your school
district offers special help for young parents, the name of
the program may be entirely different. Call your district.

Learning About Special Programs

Sue's "special program" is similar to programs available in many school districts across the United States under the School to Work Opportunities Act. Ask your school district about these School to Work opportunities or, in California, "School to Career" programs. Through these programs, community-based training will be provided as well as in-class instruction. The focus is on basic skills as well as job training.

Another source for job training is JTPA (Job Training Partnership Act), which is in operation across the country. This is funded in part by local employers.

Those Who Don't Work

Sometimes I don't know about the future. It de-pends on Zaid. We'll stay together as long as he tries.

Zaid doesn't work. My step-dad is trying to get him a job. He's 22, and he doesn't have much education at all. In the past he's had little odd jobs here and there.

I'd like him to get a job, something to keep him busy. My step-dad has a business, and he's willing to teach Zaid. I think he needs something to keep his mind occupied and to boost his self-esteem.

Tameka, 17/Zaid, 22 (Chantilly, 6 months)

Indeed Zaid needs to get a job. Tameka is wise to under-stand that he needs to work for his own sake. Zaid also must realize that his family needs his financial help. Pro-viding half the support for his child is his responsibility.

No longer do the majority of teens think the man should support his family by himself while the woman stays home. Only one-third of the men and one-fifth of the women in the Marriage Expectations Survey think the husband should "absolutely" or "probably" earn most of the money. Two-thirds of the men and almost four-fifths of the women feel both partners should be working and providing financial support for their family.

Several of the young women I interviewed spoke of partners who didn't work and who seldom took responsibility for their child or their home. Traci has that problem:

I feel a lot of pressure. I'm supporting Elias by myself. I buy the diapers, everything. I get real frustrated because Wes isn't helping out.

It was a 7 a.m. job, and he didn't like to get up that early.

We're getting counseling, and we talk about it there. He says when he gets a job, he'll help out. I figure when he gets his job, everything will be okay. My mom and I both work days now. Elias goes to day care, or sometimes Wes will stay home with him.

Money is a problem. I pay for the electricity and the phone bill. I make only $5 an hour, so I don't have much. My mom helps me out. I keep trying to budget my money, but it doesn't work out.

The more I pressure Wes, the more he isn't going to get a job. He worked at a canning plant here, but he's not one to get up early in the morning. It was a 7 a.m. job, and he didn't like to get up that early. When I had to get to work at 5:30, he'd take me, and then he wouldn't make it to his job. Then one day he didn't call in, and he got fired.

There are days when I just want to kick him out the door. I've done that before because I'm tired of supporting him, myself, and Elias. It's hard.

Traci, 16/Wesley, 20 (Elias, 20 months)

Wes commented:

I know I have to get a job, but I don't really want one. I've worked at several jobs, but I didn't like any of them.

Both Parents Need Job Skills

Neither Wes nor Traci has finished high school. Traci said wistfully:

My ideal would be both of us working but me getting off earlier and having supper ready when Wes gets here. I'd like him to have a better job than me. I could handle that. I think it would make him happier and give me more time to work at home.

The real problem here, of course, is not who makes the most money or has the better job. It's how, as a couple, they can make enough to support themselves and their child. Wes can't with no job at all, and Traci can't with a $5/hour job.

Wes and Traci need to talk to a job training counselor at their local community college or adult school. Or Traci, who is only 16, might be able to figure out a way to get back to high school. Her local high school recently opened a childcare center.

Both Traci and Wes need to check out learning programs available for young parents. She might qualify for a grant while she continues her education, a grant that might provide nearly as much financial help as her low-paying job. Or perhaps she could continue to work part-time while she's in school.

Wes mentioned thinking about Job Corps, then not getting around to applying. He needs to talk to a good job training counselor and learn as much as possible about available opportunities. Job Corps might be an excellent way for him to become job-ready. He might find, however, that he has to get over his dislike of getting up early!

Job Corps is especially for those who have dropped out of school. It is another program which provides job training. In some communities, housing is provided. In other places, Job Corps is a day program.

In your grandfather's time, a person who wanted to work could usually find employment. Today, a high school diploma is required for most jobs, and often it's not enough. Traci and Wes have a difficult situation, but there are opportunities out there. It takes hard work to learn about those opportunities, and much more hard work to get the job training, then the good job they each need. Hardest work of all, probably, is keeping that good job.

Baby Inspires Hard Work

For many young parents, having a baby is their major inspiration for working hard:

> *A friend of mine has a year-old baby. Before I even knew Janita was pregnant, he told me, "When I realized my girlfriend was pregnant, I was scared and I felt trapped. Then once the baby was born, I'd look at her and think, 'Just look at what you brought into this world.' Looking at that baby gave me the inspiration to get up, put some clothes on, and go out and look for a job."*
>
> *That's what I do. I look at Janita's belly, and that's what keeps me going with that part-time job and going to school. That kid will kick you out the door to get a job.*

> Elijah, 19/Janita, 16

Johnny Angel, too, is working hard to support his wife and child, and to continue his education at the same time:

"That kid will kick you out the door to get a job."

Davina and the baby got me a lot more serious about the future and my whole life. I want to give them the things they need. I want Davina to continue on with school.

I'm a part-time college student and part-time grocery clerk. I'm very serious now about my education and finishing school. That's the only way you can do it nowadays.

We'll probably both have to work, and we'll have some hard times.

Johnny Angel, 19/Davina, 19 (Valizette, 11 days)

Some companies, such as Kaiser Permanente, have good training programs:

I hope to graduate in June, then work at Kaiser this summer. I'll probably start in patient filing, and once I get in, I can switch to other departments. I want to go into nursing.

Kaiser pays for you to go to school, like $2500 a year. They have a lot of benefits.

Danielle, 17/Jordan, 23

Ask your school vocational counselor for information about training programs in your area. Ask about programs under the Carl Perkins Sex Equity funding. Also ask about new programs because these change frequently with new legislation dealing with job training.

If you're a woman, look at non-traditional job possibilities (jobs such as auto mechanic that are usually held by men) as well as the typically female areas such as office work, waitressing, hair styling, etc. Those non-traditional jobs are likely to pay better.

High school credit for work experience is available through area vocational schools, adult school, community college, and your high school. Check with your counselor.

Setting Goals

Whether you already have a good job or you've dropped out of school and have no skills, setting goals can help you. Start by having a needs assessment evaluation. Ask your school or vocational counselor how you can have this done. Your long-term vocational goals should be based on your needs assessment results. You want to work toward a career which you will enjoy and which will provide the income you need to support yourself and your family. A needs assessment can help you find the right career for you.

Also set short-term goals for yourself. If you've dropped out of school, how soon can you return to classes? Your first goal might be to learn about the different ways you could earn a high school diploma in your community. Perhaps an alternative school would meet your needs best. If you're at least 18, you may be able to complete your high school requirements at your community college. That's also a good place to check out job training opportunities.

Having job experience is often a help in getting another job. It's frustrating to apply for jobs, only to be told, "Sorry. We hire only experienced workers." If no one will hire you, how do you get experience?

The answer is to get job experience however you can. If it's at McDonald's, fine. Do the best job you can, let your employer know how reliable you are, and how well you work with other people. If you do a great job, and you're there when you're supposed to be, before long you'll have that coveted job experience.

As you're working part-time and continuing your education, find out about opportunities for more job training. As mentioned before, there are subsidized programs that provide some financial support for teen parents who want to continue school and/or get job training. There may be child care available, money for transportation, etc.

As you set your goals, figure out the steps you must take to reach them. Elijah's advice may help you hang in there:

> *If you're a teen mother or father, you don't have time to think about yourself. This is no time to be a cop-out. There's no time to say, "I can't find a job." Once you decide you're pregnant, or your girlfriend's pregnant, and you decide to have the baby, you have to discipline yourself. You have to do everything possible for your child.*
>
> *Just look at that child and say, "I'm going to do everything I can to take care of you the best I can."*
>
> Elijah

She needs good food for the baby as well as herself.

CHAPTER 8

Pregnancy
Brings Change

Myra's pregnancy opened my eyes to what I have coming. I'm young, I'm having a kid at 18. That's not right. I want to be able to give my kid everything on my own the way my dad did for me. It's not right, but it's done. It's not a bad thing—I don't feel it's the end of life, although I'd rather have had him when I was financially stable with my own house and car.

We have to understand this isn't a perfect world. We'll grow up together.

Sam, 18/Myra, 17

A pregnancy, especially if it's unplanned, may be hard on a couple's relationship. She may not feel well. Morning sickness affects some women during the first three months of pregnancy, and for a few, throughout the pregnancy. Others feel fine physically.

Expect Mood Swings

Nearly all pregnant women experience mood swings.
Even if she wanted to get pregnant and she's delighted
about the coming baby, she will have periods of depression.
This is caused to a great extent by hormonal changes
occurring in her body because of the pregnancy. She may
cry for no reason. At other times she may snap at her
partner, and he'll wonder what got into her.

> *We argue all the time. But I look at it like this.
> She's real moody since she got pregnant. I called my
> brother because he just went through a pregnancy. I
> asked, "What can I do? She's arguing for no reason."*
>
> *He said, "Whenever she starts an argument, just be
> quiet, say nothing." Before Janita was pregnant, we'd
> argue and I'd be the ringleader. I'd tell her to get her
> feelings out.*
>
> *I don't think just leaving is good at all. I tried it
> once, and when I came back, it was worse. "Why did
> you leave? That shows how much you care. We get
> into an argument and you just leave." I understand
> that it's good to get it out face-to-face. But things are
> different now while she's pregnant.*
>
> Elijah, 19/Janita, 16

If the father can be involved in the visits to the doctor
and in reading about the changes brought about by pregnancy, he'll find it easier to understand these mood swings.
If they can attend prepared childbirth classes together and if
he can coach her during labor and delivery, the baby will
seem more "ours" than "hers."

> *I helped as much as I could. We went to Lamaze
> class together, and I coached her during labor and
> delivery. It's a lot of work—you don't know that from
> health class. It's something you have to experience*

*yourself. I have so much respect for Marlene and for
any woman who goes through that.*

*After Amber Marie was born, it was pretty busy
and exciting. It was real neat, but kind of inconve-
nient. We were waking up constantly in the middle of
the night. We were tired!*

Jeremy, 19/Marlene, 16 (Amber Marie, 7 months)

*I liked Alfonso being here for me when I was
pregnant. When my legs hurt, he'd rub them. He
rubbed my back, and he'd talk to the baby. He helped
me a lot. I liked my time when I was pregnant and he
was here. What I didn't like was when he was gone,
and I'd get all emotional because he wasn't here.*

Arlene, 14/Alfonso, 16 (Sylvia, 4 months)

Elijah understands that pregnancy is not forever, and that
his and Janita's relationship will return to normal—more or
less—after their baby is born:

*When the baby's born, we'll have a chance to send
it to the grandparents for the weekend and have an
intimate time. There's no intimate time now because
Janita's pregnant, and she's too hot or tired or sick.
She's giving her body away to the baby for these
months, and I'm thankful for what she's doing.*

Elijah

He Wasn't Supportive

Enrique wasn't as supportive during her first pregnancy
as Selia would have liked. They discussed those months,
months in which they faced some of the problems often
encountered by pregnant teenage couples:

Selia: *Pregnancy was not a surprise. It was
planned. We both said we wanted a baby. We were
both seniors. He was born on my commencement day.*

I got my diploma, but I didn't get to walk down the aisle. He came a month early.

Enrique: *After the baby was born, Selia stayed with her mother. Our relationship was not as strong as it should have been. During her pregnancy I wasn't working as a team. She would get sick and I wouldn't know what to say.*

Selia: *He shied away.*

Enrique: *I wasn't expecting her emotions. I wasn't walking with her.*

Selia: *He didn't understand, and I didn't either. I felt unattractive, I felt it's all my fault. I was extremely depressed. I felt deserted. I didn't know what to do. For a month after Riquie was born, I didn't want anything to do with Enrique because if he deserted me before Riquie was born, why would I trust him now? Then he asked me to marry him, and we did. He took care of Riquie financially, but no emotional support at first.*

Enrique: *I didn't understand the emotions that were going on. I was taking counseling. They started showing me different things but I didn't understand. They were teaching me how I should act around Selia when she would go through the emotional stages. But being hard-headed, I didn't listen. It kind of broke us apart. But eventually we got stronger. I had promised her I would never leave her, and I never did even as she was going through these changes.*

Selia: *He was there when I went into labor. I never had Lamaze so the nurses gave him a ten-minute lesson, and he went through it with me. That night kind of made up for the eight months. The hospital was eight miles away, and he got there by bus in the middle of the night. He didn't sleep it out.*

Selia, 19/Enrique, 19 (Riquie, 11 months)

She especially needs her partner's support during pregnancy.

Better the Second Time

Selia and Enrique were four months into their second pregnancy when I interviewed them. This time, Enrique is providing much more support to his wife:

Selia: *After birth I discovered my body had taken a toll I didn't expect, and for a month after Riquie was born I didn't want to have anything to do with Enrique. He would say he was sorry, and I finally said okay. For this pregnancy he has done a complete 200° turnaround.*

My advice to the man is to read with the woman, especially if it's her first pregnancy. I would show Enrique the books, and he told me he didn't feel as if it was real yet. If the guy doesn't care, then he should act like he does. It will make her feel better.

Enrique: *My advice for the fathers—the woman goes through the most, but for teenage fathers, stay with the woman, even if you're going through all kinds of trials and tribulations. I would encourage*

*teenage fathers to be more honest. Fathers go
through the pregnancy, too. It's hard for the father,
too. He needs to talk to his mate about how he feels
about this situation and what changes he's going
through emotionally.*

*At first I worried about the financial part, but I
knew I'm a workaholic and I could get a job.*

*If you're about to be a father. . . first of all, you
have to be mature if you're going to be a father. You
have a whole lot of responsibility ahead of you. You
have to take care of yourself, and also that woman
and the child.*

If Pregnancy Means Moving

Celina, then 16, moved in with Scott, 19, and his family
soon after she became pregnant. She shared some difficulties she faced in adjusting to a new family at this time:

*Almost as soon as Scott and I knew I was pregnant,
I moved in with him and his parents. They didn't
know I was pregnant, and he took two months to tell
them. He knew he could count on his mom, but he
took forever to tell his dad because he's an alcoholic.
Scott thought his dad would beat him up. He waited
until his dad was in a happy mood, and he told him.
His dad took it okay, and said he wished we had told
him a long time ago.*

*It was hard living with Scott's family. I didn't feel
comfortable. His mom wouldn't let me cook or clean.
She kept telling me to make myself at home, but she
wouldn't let me help. I'm used to cleaning and cooking, but his mom would say, "No, you don't have to
do it," and I would feel bad because I wanted to help.*

*I came back home about three months before
Melanie was born. I was homesick. I needed my*

*family, and we weren't married at that time. Also, I
wasn't eating well at Scott's house because his mom
really didn't have time to cook. I was afraid to cook
whatever I wanted because they might think I'm
weird. I'd wake up hungry, and I'd be too
embarrassed to go to the kitchen and eat.*

*I wasn't used to their food, and sometimes I didn't
like what she cooked. I'm used to Mexican food.
They're white, and they'd make different foods like
steak, and I'm not used to that.*

Celina, 17/Scott, 20 (Melanie, 6 weeks)

The moodiness and nausea often experienced by a
woman during early pregnancy make this an especially
difficult time to adjust to a new family. If she's young and
has never lived away from her parents before, she may be
quite homesick, no matter how much she loves her partner.
To add to her difficulties, her parents (and his) may be
upset about the pregnancy.

Sharing her feelings with her partner and with his parents may help. She needs to be open about her needs
including her nutritional needs. She must eat the right foods
to help her baby develop into a healthy newborn.

Prenatal Care Is Essential

If you're pregnant, do you already know how important
it is to see your doctor as early as possible in your pregnancy? You need to see your doctor at least once each
month, more often during your last trimester. Even if you
feel wonderful, don't put off these visits. They're an
important part of having a healthy baby.

If you are the "pregnant" man, you have a very important role in your child's development. Can you go with
your partner to see her doctor? Read the pamphlets and
books she'll be reading about pregnancy. Be aware of the

*If you are the father, you can encourage your partner to eat
the foods she and your baby need during pregnancy.*

size and activity of your child at each stage of pregnancy.
This will make your baby seem more real to you.

How can you help your partner produce a healthy baby?
There are lots of things you can do:

You can help her eat the nutritious foods she and your
baby need at this important time.

Do all you can to help her stay completely away from
alcohol and all drugs except those prescribed by her doctor.
If you don't drink or take drugs, she may find it easier
to abstain.

> *I drink every once in awhile. But when Mitzuko got
> pregnant, and she couldn't drink, I wasn't going to
> drink around her. So I left it alone.*
>   Maurice, 21/Mitzuko, 16 (Lana, 14 months)

If she smokes, strongly encourage her to stop as early in pregnancy as possible. If you don't smoke, she may be more able to forget the cigarettes. Besides, second-hand smoke is also a risk to that unborn child of yours.

> *I used to smoke but I stopped in my second month of pregnancy. Elijah couldn't stand it. He used to hide my cigarettes—he'd drive me crazy. He got me to quit, and I don't think I'll start again.*
>
> Janita, 16/Elijah, 19

For more information about the physical and emotional changes brought about by pregnancy, and for suggestions on producing a healthy baby, see *Teens Parenting:Your Pregnancy and Newborn Journey* (1991: Morning Glory Press).

For more detailed information from the father's perspective, see chapters 2-5, *Teen Dads: Rights, Responsibilities and Joys* (1993: Morning Glory Press).

Concerns After Delivery

Celina, who discussed her difficulties in living with Scott's family early in her pregnancy, expressed another concern after their child was born. She's worried about the effect of second-hand smoke on their baby:

> *Scott's dad smokes and so does Scott, and I don't think it's a good environment for our baby. Scott would never smoke around me, but still, that smell on him makes me sick. I tell him to wash his hands and brush his teeth before he holds the baby.*
>
> Celina

Celina is well aware of the research showing the bad effects for babies and children when someone in their home smokes. A child living with second-hand smoke is more likely to develop asthma and other respiratory diseases.

Celina wants their child to have the best chance possible at a healthy life.

This is a difficult situation. Would Scott and his father be willing to smoke outside? Many smokers who feel they can't quit are making this concession for the sake of their child's health. If her father-in-law insists on smoking around the baby, Celina may decide to keep Melanie in their room as much as possible—assuming she can persuade Scott not to smoke in there.

The father-in-law's smoking may be an incentive for Celina and Scott to work toward moving into an apartment of their own as soon as possible.

Childbirth and Sexual Feelings

Especially when I was pregnant, it was like "No!" He would bug me, and I didn't want him to get mad because of that. He'd ask me after birth and I would say, "No way."

Brenda, 17/Santos, 18 (Lydia, 4 months)

Childbirth often has a strong effect on a woman's sex drive. Her partner may find it hard to understand why she is so tired and uninterested. Her doctor probably recommends she not have intercourse until six weeks after childbirth— yet her partner may not understand why they should wait.

Her sex drive is probably very low, quite different from his at this time. Sometimes it's hard to work these things out.

Mary Jane, 16, and Carl, 18, have twin daughters. Two months after they were born, she said:

I just don't feel very sexy. This makes Carl mad. He says that I don't love him, but that's ridiculous. Of course I love him. But I don't feel like having sex.

Twice we've gotten a sitter to take the girls out for a couple of hours. I felt different then. That was nice.

Mary Jane is undoubtedly exhausted. Taking care of one baby is more than enough for most people, but twins? Sometimes hiring a baby-sitter and sending that person *out* with the baby can do wonders for a couple's relationship.

Fear of getting pregnant again can make one feel very unsexy. Breastfeeding can't be relied on to keep you from having another baby.

Your doctor may recommend the Depo-Provera three-month injection six weeks after your baby is born, even if you're breastfeeding. A condom and foam used together provide a good method until you talk with your doctor or go to a family planning clinic. See chapter 10 for more information about planning your family.

Pain during lovemaking is a real problem for many new mothers, especially if they had stitches after delivery. If she's afraid sex will hurt, she'll feel anxious. This can start a vicious cycle because anxiety and tension make it worse.

Some women have vaginal dryness if they're breast-feeding. This may make intercourse painful, or at least uncomfortable. Using a water-base lubricant such as K-Y Jelly should help.

Saying "No" is, of course, everyone's right. If both partners love and want to please each other, they'll talk about their feelings. They'll share their thinking whether it's "I'm feeling terribly horny right now" or "This baby has made me so tired that the last thing I want to think about is sex." If each of you truly listen to the other, you'll find caring solutions that work for both of you.

This, Too, Will Pass

Jean Brunelli, nurse in the Tracy Infant Center, Cerritos, California, talked about the probable differences in sex drive between a new mother and a new father. "I know this can become a problem with young couples. Of course we

support the young mother's right not to feel sexy after
childbirth.

"We also need to remember that young guys talk a lot
about sex and feel very competitive. They like to brag
about their sexual prowess. At the same time, this young
man is being turned away by his woman, which may
actually make him feel abnormal. He can't get her to do it
when everybody else is doing it all the time."

*He has a hard time understanding how you feel
when you're pregnant and after the baby is born—
why you don't want to have sex all the time. He
doesn't understand why you get upset real easy, why
you cry over nothing. We talk about it a lot. We can
communicate. But it's hard.*

Melodie, 17/Brett, 19 (Skylar, 2 months)

"There is no simple solution. Best thing is for the young
couple to talk about it," Ms. Brunelli continued. "He should
be able to say to her, 'It makes me feel weird. Every guy I
know seems to be having sex all the time. Why can't we?'

"Maybe she needs to be able to say, 'This is just a short
time in our lives. It's a part of the whole experience of
having a baby. This will change.'

"If they're able to have some time alone, and if she gets
more rest, this stage should end more quickly," Ms.
Brunelli concluded.

*The sex is still there—when it doesn't get inter-
rupted by a screaming baby. There's never enough
time for it, or I'm too tired. One day it will be back
to normal.*

Tameka, 17/Zaid, 22 (Chantilly, 6 months)

If you and your partner have not had a baby yet, be
aware that these problems may occur. Before your baby is
born is a time when you probably will feel very close and

warm, and you won't yet have the distractions of constant baby care. This is the best time to start talking about how you'll handle the pressures that almost always occur after delivery.

Ms. Brunelli also talked about the other pressures young fathers may be feeling. "Perhaps a few months ago his paycheck was supposed to support himself and his car. Now with that same paycheck he's trying to support his wife and child. This often causes a lot of stress. Many young men look at sex as a stress reducer, and if they can't do that, they're really puzzled."

Sharing Baby Care Helps

Incidentally, this may be another reason for dad to be very involved in parenting his infant. Parenting at this stage means getting up night after night with the baby, changing diapers time after time, rocking her, talking to her, loving her, feeding her. Dad can play a full-parent role in everything except breastfeeding.

If he's acting like a parent—which means not expecting mom to do all the work with the baby—he may find a bonus. Mom is much more likely to be interested in sex sooner than she would be if she were responsible for all the tremendous amount of work associated with taking care of a tiny infant.

His baby will also appreciate him more if he's deeply involved.

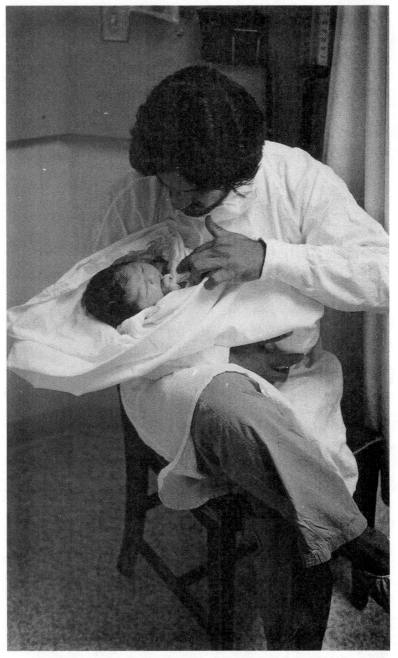

You'll love baby dearly—but he will cause lots of commotion!

CHAPTER 9

Child-Created Commotion

Having a baby changed my life and kept me from running around, doing guy stuff. I miss it somewhat.

Kenny, 17/Misty, 18 (Damian, 11 months)

If you have a baby, it's nice to live with each other so you can raise the baby together. When Alfonso isn't here and she laughs, I want to call him and say, "She laughed! She laughed for the first time!" If he were living someplace else, he'd miss that.

She's a daddy's girl. When he walks in the door, she has a big old smile.

Arlene, 14/Alfonso, 16 (Sylvia, 4 months)

Right now we're both going through a lot of changes. We have this new little person to work with. She's changing. My wife is changing, I'm changing, and we both get frustrated, especially me.

Being up late at night, working, school, trying to help my wife. Sometimes it gets hard and I tend to get frustrated.

We keep it under control. It's a whole new ball game. Like I used to tell Davina, I considered her my teammate, and together we could take on the world. Now we have a new little teammate, and we're trying to work her in.

Every time I look at Valizette, it's worth it. Every time I see Davina look at her, she's worth it. I think the most important thing we're giving her right now are two loving parents.

It's like being thrown into some kind of game without instructions. If the child doesn't have both parents giving her support, she loses out.

Johnny Angel, 19/Davina, 19 (Valizette, 11 days)

A child creates lots of commotion. There's no doubt about it. Having a baby changes a couple's lifestyle. Even if their baby is good—which to most people means a relaxed infant who sleeps a lot—the parents are going to be very busy. If they have a fussy baby, they'll wonder if they ever again will get a good night's sleep.

An infant takes lots of time, but generally she'll sleep many hours each day and, hopefully, each night. As your infant develops into a toddler, she'll make even greater changes in your lives.

Marriage Relationship Is Primary

In a way, the baby has brought us closer together, and in a way, she hasn't. We're closer because we have something to share. But we don't have time together any more.

Now when Alfonso comes home, it's "Hi, Sylvia,"

and she gets the hugs and kisses. I'm not jealous, but
it just isn't the same.

Arlene

New parents are generally astonished at how much time
it takes to care for a baby. Sure, some new babies sleep a
lot. But some don't. And even when he's sleeping, someone has to do the laundry, prepare his formula (unless he's
breastfed), and complete a seemingly endless series
of tasks.

We're together a lot, but now that we have the
baby, we don't spend as much time with each other.
We don't really have any free time to ourselves. She's
made both of us grow up a lot.

I'm still young, and I was like a little kid. Now that
I have the baby, I have to be like an adult. I have
responsibilities. I have to take care of another person
besides. I kind of miss the freedom.

Summer, 15/Daesun, 20 (Cecelia, 9 months)

You and your partner need times alone together without
your child. It's important to remember always that, even
though you have a child, your relationship with your spouse
is still your primary relationship. Eighteen years of being
responsible for a child is a long time. But if your marriage
is forever, you'll have a lot of years left after your children
are gone.

I think you have to work on your marriage because
the kids will grow up and move away and you'll still
have your husband or wife. I think a lot of people get
married and have kids, then put their whole focus on
their kids. They kind of lose touch with each other.
You need to go out by yourselves, spend some time
without the kids.

Betsy, 17/Larry, 18

It takes a lot of planning and effort to make time for each other when you have a child—especially if you're both working and/or going to school. It's important, however, that you find time together. It's important to your child that your relationship continues to grow in caring and in love.

Satisfying Three People's Needs

We've lived together for nearly a year. At first it was all new, and it seemed special. We had time to share together. We were a family together in the same house. At first I thought it would be easier for me, for the baby, and for Mitzuko, for all of us, if we were together as a family. That's how we were both raised, that families should stay together. It made me feel good, like I was doing the right thing.

After awhile . . . you hear all the horror stories of having a baby. It's no horror story, but having a crying baby in the middle of the night, getting up in the middle of the night, is no joke.

First it was like a little game. I was happy with the changes. If nobody else wanted to hold Lana, I was happy to hold her. Then, as time went on, "Do I have to change her diaper?" "Do you really want me to hold her this minute?"

Maurice, 21/Mitzuko, 16 (Lana, 14 months)

If you're married or living with a partner, you know how much adjusting it takes to learn to live with another person. You each have needs, and it's hard to satisfy each other's needs often enough.

If you add a baby to your relationship, the changes multiply. While your spouse probably makes at least some effort to please you, to satisfy your needs, your baby will do no such thing. A baby's needs are for satisfying *now*— with no regard for how you're feeling.

Newborns Don't Spoil

Most childcare experts today tell us we can't spoil a baby during the first few months after birth. If a tiny baby is hungry, she is in actual physical pain. She needs to be fed at once.

If you're sure she's not hungry and you know she's dry, but she continues crying, she probably is lonely. Leaving her to cry it out in her crib is not the way to go. Comfort her and love her.

Of course no one can keep a baby satisfied all the time. If you expect that of yourself, you're doomed to disappointment and to feeling extremely tired. But you and your baby's other parent will want to do your best to give your baby what she needs—which includes lots of loving.

Think about what that goal means. During the first weeks it may mean feeding the baby every couple of hours. By the time you've changed his diaper, burped him, and rocked him, in addition to the feeding, you've spent an hour. You'll feel as though you're spending *all* your time with the baby—and you may be right.

What do you think this might do to your relationship with your partner? In the Marriage Expectations Survey, a majority of the respondents thought it was very important for a couple to spend most of their spare time with each other. In a good relationship, we usually want to spend lots of time together.

A baby's birth can change all that.

The baby is very time consuming. I lived carefree. Now that she's here, my daytime, my nighttime, all rotate around her and Angela. I feel more responsibilities.

Juan, 18/Angela, 16 (Vaneza, 7 months)

You and your partner may decide to focus on each other during the brief times you do have alone at this busy time.

Dad Is Full Parent, Too

Of course dad is a full parent, too. Bonding means the very special tie that develops between a baby and his mother and, hopefully, father. It depends on lots of closeness between the baby and each parent.

> *Vincent loves little Saulo. He talks to him, he carries him, he feeds him, he changes him. I feel really nice when his father is taking care of him. I know he loves him.*
>
> *No matter how much you love your baby, you get tired of the responsibility, especially when you're young. Sometimes I think, "God, I'm young. Why did I get myself into this?" But it all pays off when he gets his first tooth or starts walking.*
>
> Karina, 16/Vincent, 20 (Saulo, 7 months)

Many young mothers report that their partners don't "like" to change diapers. Naturally. Who really "likes" to change a diaper?

But diaper changing has its positive side—and not only because baby needs a dry diaper. This is a wonderful time to communicate with your baby. If dad doesn't do his share of changing, not only is mother likely to be too busy, but, more important, dad is missing out on an enjoyable part of parenting.

Even if mom is breastfeeding, dad, when he's home, can still share in all the other care of the baby—the rocking, the burping, the diaper-changing, the daily bath. Incidentally, there is no reason a baby needs a bath in the morning instead of in the evening. The best time is when both parents can either share in this undertaking or take turns. Baby's bath is a very special time for mom and dad.

The traditional role-playing of mom taking care of the baby while dad works is not followed by many young

families today. In fact, it's amazing that child care is ever
assumed to be "woman's work." If parenting is a positive
experience (and we must think it is or so many of us
wouldn't continue having babies), then both parents deserve to share the joys involved. If it's a lot of hard work
(we all know it is), certainly both parents should share
that burden.

> *I was laid off last spring when Lana was five
> months old. Mitzuko had summer school, so we
> decided I would stay home with the baby while she
> went to school.*
>
> *So I stayed home and watched Lana every day. At
> first it was horrible because Mitzuko nursed, and
> Lana wouldn't take the bottle for awhile. She would
> hardly eat, and she was crying all the time until
> Mitzuko got home. Then everything was okay.*
>
> *When Mitzuko came home, I'd feel like, "It's your
> turn." It gave me a good perspective on it because I
> hear women all the time saying staying home with the
> baby is like a 24-hour job. I experienced it for myself.
> It's probably the hardest job I ever had.*
>
> Maurice

Baby Needs Both Parents' Attention

Most people still think it's preferable for children to
have two parents. When both parents are in the home, it's a
little silly for that child to see one of them for only a few
minutes of play each day. Baby wants and needs real
involvement with both parents.

> *Both parents need to be good role models. I missed
> that when I was growing up. I really wanted my father
> around a lot, but the only male I had in my life was
> my uncle. He taught me a lot, but it's still not the*

*same as having a father. I missed that. Everything I
missed doing with my father, I'm going to do it with
my children. I don't think kids should have to go
outside the family to find a role model.*

Enrique, 19/Selia, 19 (Riquie, 11 months)

Parenting involves a lot more than making babies. Some
men get excited at the idea of being a father, but don't want
to be actively involved in parenting. They don't support
their partners or their babies. They don't help with child
care. Planting the sperm, they seem to think, is doing
their share.

Other fathers feel quite differently:

*I'm trying to change the stereotype of teenage
fathers. It's like all fathers were never there. I feel my
child didn't ask to be born. My child deserves a
mother and a father, and the mother and father
should be equal.*

*I feel like if I laid down with her to make the baby,
I should be there. I want to be there 100 percent for
my child. I'm sick of everything being the mom and
the baby in the media. I grew up with just my mom,
and I don't want it to be like that. I want to be there
for my baby.*

*Spend time with your kid even if you don't have a
dime in your pocket. Be there for your kid. Hug him.
That's more important than anything.*

Elijah, 19/Janita, 16

A lot of men, like Elijah, work hard at becoming caring,
responsible fathers. If you are a mother, you may have a
partner who is working hard to support you. He may have
wanted a baby. If he didn't, he figures if you're pregnant or
you already have a child, he'll handle the situation as best
he can.

Helping Dad Feel Capable

Special to mom: If he's never been around babies very much, he may need a lot of extra encouragement.

First, make sure he knows you welcome his active involvement in the care of this baby. *Start as soon after the baby is born as possible.* If he coaches you through labor and is there with you when your baby is born, he'll have a good start in fathering. Some hospitals let the father stay in the room with the mother and baby as much as he wishes throughout their hospital stay.

If dad says he doesn't know how to hold a tiny baby, show him. Be reassuring. If he insists he can't diaper a baby, help him learn.

Help him understand that the more he shares in caring for his child, the more he'll also share in the joys of parenting this child. And your child is worth the effort!

Good Parenting Takes Learning

Most of us aren't born to be "good" parents. It may be natural to love one's baby, but knowing what that baby needs as he develops is not automatic.

Even if you have helped care for little brothers and sisters, you'd be wise to learn as much as possible about babies before yours is born. If you can learn together as a couple, you'll have fewer disagreements later over different approaches to childrearing. If only one of you can take a child care class, that one should share as much of the class discussions as possible with the other.

Hopefully, mom and dad agree on such basic things as nutrition, discipline, and the importance of routines in a child's life. If so, they will find caring for their child is a far easier task. If they argue over these matters, their child will learn to play one parent against the other. In this game, nobody wins.

Different Views on Discipline

Kent doesn't know how to take care of Satira very well. He provides the money. Once in a while, and this is very rare, I want to take a nap in the afternoon. Then he takes care of Satira. But he wants her confined to one spot while I let her explore as long as she doesn't get hurt. But he knows he's right. He doesn't want to listen to me. He doesn't care much about what I think.

Stephanie, 18/Kent, 20 (Satira, 8 months)

We don't agree on discipline. He wants to spank Sergio, but I don't think that's a good way. My parents spanked me, and I didn't learn anything except rebelling. I get further talking with him, but Caesar says that's too easy.

Carman, 16/Caesar, 21 (Sergio, 2 years)

I had to learn about disciplining Larissa. All I knew was to hit her, and I didn't want to do that. I had to learn how to talk with her and let her know I loved her. My dad never used the word "love."

Shanna helped me a lot, and talking with Paul at Teen Parenting taught me a lot. We try not to ever spank Larissa. She'll take a nap if she's cranky. She's a nice little kid. I like to take her places, and she has bonded with me.

Randy, 21/Shanna, 18 (Larissa, 15 months)

When Kianna gets into stuff, I grab her, or put things up higher. We don't slap her hands.

Antonio, 17/Elaine, 19 (Kianna, 13 months; Sarah, 2 months)

We have different views on what is right for Daron. Nathan says I give in too much. I think he gives in too much sometimes. We talk about it and it's over.

You can't have one parent say "Yes" and the other parent say "No" because the child knows which one to see to always get his way. We don't want him like that.

Katelynn, 17/Nathan, 20 (Daron, 2 1/2 years)

We had lots of arguments about our son. We were both too extreme. James would yell at Jacari and want to hit him. That would make me want to baby him because I'd feel bad because James was mad at him.

Angelica, 18 (Jacari, 3 years)

Children need freedom *and* discipline. If each of these couples could take a good parenting class together, the discussions there might help them. Each might learn how important it is for little kids to have times and places to play freely. They also might learn more about discipline as teaching, not punishing.

*Babies need freedom **and** discipline.*

Parents need to develop together a consistent pattern of discipline for their child as well as allowing him the freedom he needs.

Studying about children together will help you and your partner understand your children's needs. Talk to each other about your opinions and your feelings concerning child care. If you don't agree, some compromise should be possible.

For a more detailed description of life with small children, see the *Teens Parenting* series: *Your Baby's First Year, The Challenge of Toddlers,* and *Discipline from Birth to Three* (1991: Morning Glory Press). Based on interviews with teenage parents, these books cover thoroughly the many aspects of baby and child care. Emphasis is on the special needs of very young parents. *Teen Dads: Rights, Responsibilities and Joys* (1993: Morning Glory Press) focuses on parenting from the father's perspective.

Grandparents Get in the Act

Sometimes parents agree with each other on childrearing methods, but don't like the way their child's grandparents treat him. If the young family is living with grandma and grandpa, this will be especially hard to deal with.

When Sergio started crawling, it was hard. We were living with Caesar's parents. They had stairs, and I felt they were dangerous for Sergio. Anything I put up so he wouldn't get it, they would just put back down. To them, those things were not dangerous.

So I supervised a lot. I didn't want to talk about it with them. Not only was I not paying rent, but I didn't want to complain about everything.

Carman

I have to chase Liana all over the place. When I say "No," she thinks I'm funny. And it's harder because Ryan's mom won't let me put things up away from her. She says you just have to watch her.

Like the tablecloth. She pulls it, and there's a vase on there. And the cords, they won't change them.

When she gets into things, I try to move her and get her something else to do. Or I start playing with her.

Conya, 19/Ryan, 21 (Liana, 11 months)

If you live in your parents' home, or in your partner's parents' home, in some ways you're still under their control. Yet you also know you need to be in charge of your own baby. How do you handle the disagreements over child care?

First, be sure you're doing a good job of caring for your baby. Be as informed as possible about child care in general, and especially about your own child's needs.

Then, if the grandparents disagree with what you're doing, talk about your reasons for thinking as you do. Explain why you think you can't spoil an infant, for example. Tell them why you want to satisfy her needs as completely as possible during these early months. If you and your partner are in agreement, your parents may be more interested in your viewpoints.

Remember, too, that your parents have had experience in caring for at least one baby—you—and the results are pretty good! Their experience may be very helpful to you and your partner as you get acquainted with your new baby and his needs.

As you and your partner work with that new little person, don't forget to care for and love each other. Your baby needs you both, and you both want to keep your love for each other alive for yourselves and your child.

Sometimes it's hard to talk about birth control.

CHAPTER 10

Your Next Baby — When?

We never used birth control. It surprised me that I didn't get pregnant right away. After the first three months I thought I was safe. I thought I couldn't get pregnant.

Then when it turned out I was, I was worried and scared. My mother was very supportive although she told me it was wrong.

I believed everything Brad told me. He said he had been with two other people, and had used a condom with both of them. During our relationship, I think he was with other people, and now I worry about that.

If you're with someone who won't use a condom and won't talk about it, maybe you shouldn't be with that person. Maybe he's not the right one.

Jessica, 15/Brad, 15 (Rodney, 4 months)

*We want another baby in three or four years. We'll
kind of get back on our future and make sure Johnny
Angel has a good job. We want to be stable before we
think about another baby.*

*I don't know yet what contraception we'll use.
We'll talk to the doctor about that. We're sure going
to use one.*

Davina, 19/Johnny Angel, 19 (Valizette, 11 days)

If you're not pregnant and you don't already have a
child, when would you and your partner like to have a
baby? Or do you want children? Some couples choose not
to have kids at all. Others decide to wait, perhaps years,
while they finish college and get a good start on their
careers.

If you already have a child, do you want more?
How soon?

You Have Choices

In your great-grandparents' time, most people felt they
had no choice in when and how many babies they had. If
they were married, they probably had babies. Some couples
had a lot of children. This worked pretty well for many
families back when most people farmed. Children were
considered an economic asset on the farm.

Today we have choices. We can decide when and how
many children we want, and even whether or not we ever
want to get pregnant. We can take responsibility for having
children when we're ready.

---

*Whether you're the man or the woman,
birth control is **your** responsibility.*

Abstinence (not having sexual intercourse) is the only
absolutely sure way to avoid pregnancy. If you aren't living

A toddler needs lots of attention.

with your partner, you may decide on this method. Most couples who are married or living together will prefer another method of birth control. Some, however, don't feel safe even with birth control:

> *Sex? There is none. It's mostly my fault, and that's our biggest problem. Judson wants to, and I just don't. It's not so much the time, but I'm just scared that I'm going to get pregnant again. I don't want to, and I get very nervous.*
>
> Aracely, 18/Judson, 27 (Chianti, 18 months)

Aracely is right. No method of birth control except abstinence can guarantee that you won't get pregnant. Several, however, if used properly every time you have sex, make it unlikely that you'll conceive.

One good choice is for the man to use a condom and the woman, foam. Using the two together is as effective at preventing pregnancy as for the woman to take the birth control pill or use an IUD (IntraUterine Device).

Most important, a condom prevents the spread of STDs (sexually transmitted diseases). Even if you're sure your partner is having sex only with you at this time, it's possible that s/he could have gotten an STD from a former partner.

A person with an STD may have no symptoms and be totally unaware of having the disease, yet can still pass it on to the partner. Using a condom makes sex safer.

Who's Responsible?

If you and your partner are sexually active, but you don't want a baby right away, who is responsible for birth control? The man or the woman? The answer is "You!" Whether you're the man or the woman, it's *your* responsibility.

If you're the man, you're risking a lot when you risk unplanned pregnancy. A baby (or, if you are already a father, another baby) would mean less freedom, much more financial responsibility, and other *big* lifestyle changes. It's your responsibility!

> *Make sure you always wear a condom. Some feel condoms don't give you the regular feeling. Some feel they aren't getting the real deal by wearing one. Others think they're just too macho for a condom.*
> *That's a dumb decision. There's too much going on these days, and they should know that.*
>   Damian, 18/Anissa, 19

If you're a woman, it's your body that must handle the pregnancy. At the right time, this can be a wonderful happening. At the wrong time, pregnancy can cause a great deal of unhappiness. One thing for sure—having a baby, whether planned or unplanned, changes your life forever.

Contraceptives for Women

The birth control pill is used by a lot of women. The pill is widely available from doctors and clinics. Your insurance or Medicaid may pay for the pill. The pill is convenient because you don't have to take it right before having sex. However, you do have to take one *every* day.

If you're breastfeeding your baby, taking the pill might cut back on your supply of milk. Talk to your doctor. It may be best to choose another contraceptive until you wean your baby to bottle or cup. Some pills, however, don't affect the making of breast milk.

Note: The pill will *not* prevent pregnancy the first month you take it. If you have sex during that time, use another contraceptive.

The pill will *not* protect either of you from STDs including AIDS.

The **IUD** is a plastic device about an inch long. It comes in various shapes.

The doctor places the IUD in the woman's uterus. Once there, it stays in for several years. It works best for women who have had only one child.

> *Your insurance may cover the cost of the implant.*

The **implant** is a low dose of birth control medicine in a capsule. The doctor puts the capsule under the skin of the woman's upper arm. It doesn't show.

Once there, it slowly releases the pregnancy-preventing medicine. This continues for at least one year. Some may

prevent pregnancy for five years. Your insurance may
cover the cost of the implant.

*Next baby? In about five years. I have the Norplant
implant—no use getting it out in a couple of years.
Besides, it's a tradition on Rick's side to have babies
every four years. That gives us a chance to give the
older child the care he needs, and for him to enjoy the
second one.*

Sue, 17/Rick, 20 (Jonathan, 7 months)

Depo-Provera Okay for Nursing Moms

*Contraception will be hard because I plan to
breastfeed so I can't have the implant. You have to be
real careful. The condoms work, but when it comes
down to sex, it's hard to wait while you put it on.*

*The pill didn't work for me because I would forget
about it.*

Janita, 16/Elijah, 19

*Depo-Provera is appropriate
for people who can't take the pill.*

Depo-Provera is a contraceptive alternative that differs
from the other methods. You are given an injection which
is effective in preventing pregnancy for three months (99
percent effective). Advantages of Depo-Provera include:

- You don't have to remember to take anything daily.
- It is appropriate for people who can't take the pill.
- Breastfeeding women can have the Depo-Provera
  injected at their six-week post-partum visit.

If you use Depo-Provera, be sure you schedule an
appointment with your doctor every three months for your
injection.

Concern About STDs

A woman who is very careful about taking the pill every day, or who uses another form of birth control, still is wise to insist on her partner using a condom because of the risk of getting an STD.

Sexually active people should be concerned about STDs. A few STDs are relatively mild while most have serious and long-lasting effects. They need immediate treatment. AIDS is an STD that causes death.

Some STDs have obvious symptoms such as big sores on the skin. Others might not show anything on the outside at all. You can't be sure by looking at someone whether or not s/he has a disease.

If you or your partner ever have any of these symptoms, see your doctor or go to a clinic:

- Painful urination (both men and women)
- Unusual discharge from the penis or vagina
- Sore or itching genitals
- Lumps or growths around genital areas
- Rashes or blisters on the genital area
- Sores on the penis, on the vulva, or in the vagina

Remember: Most STDs can be treated. Early treatment prevents serious lifelong effects. Medicaid and private insurance pay for this care, and public health departments provide free or very low cost treatment for STDs.

AIDS—An Incurable STD

AIDS (Acquired Immune Deficiency Syndrome) cannot be treated successfully. The AIDS virus makes the body unable to fight diseases, and a person with AIDS could die from any disease. Most often, cancer or pneumonia is the cause of death.

There are no early symptoms of AIDS and there is no cure. People who have AIDS are treated for their symptoms. However, they will not be cured.

In the past, some people got AIDS through blood transfusions. This is almost impossible today. Blood for transfusions is now thoroughly tested for the AIDS virus.

Today people get AIDS by:

• Having sex with an infected person

• Sharing needles with infected people

• Having sex with someone who shares needles with IV drug users

• Being infected before or during birth by mother

Talking About Birth Control

For some teens, talking about birth control is difficult. They find it an embarrassing subject. They worry that the partner will be insulted if they bring up the risk of STDs.

"I feel" messages probably will work best. "I'd feel more comfortable if you used a condom."

"I'd like to use a condom to protect both of us." Caring and concern for each other means you want to protect each other from the problems of unexpected pregnancy and from STDs.

---

*Not having enough money
to give your kids the things they need
is tough.*

If you don't already have a baby, why should you wait? You've probably already heard lots of reasons:

• You need to get your education first.

• You and your partner should have good jobs before you have a child.

If you delay your second pregnancy, you'll have more time for your first child.

- If you have a baby, you can't do the social things most teens enjoy.

The list could go on and on. The reality is that the great majority of people who have babies in their teens are poor, and stay poor as they raise their children. Giving up your teenage years is tough. Not having enough money to give your kids the things they need is even tougher.

If you're not pregnant, use birth control and wait. Hold off on the babies for awhile. A baby isn't a doll. Next baby? When Sylvia is 30! Not really. I want a baby maybe when she's 3, but I'll still be in my teens.
I don't want another baby until I'm financially ready for one. They're very expensive.

Arlene, 14/Alfonso, 16 (Sylvia, 4 months)

If You Already Have a Baby

*I'd rather have waited for the baby. We won't have
another for at least three years.*

*You should use contraception because you never
know. I want to wait because I don't want two babies
in diapers.*

Teresa, 18/Michael, 22 (Taylor, 8 months)

Why do some teen parents decide not to have another
baby right away? Celina explained the reasons she and
Scott want to wait:

*We don't want another baby until we have our own
place and until we have money. Scott wants another
baby, but he wants them three years apart.*

*I told him if we don't have all the stuff we need for
the baby, we won't have one. He wants two, and I
want three, but it depends on the money.*

Celina, 17/Scott, 20 (Melanie, 6 weeks)

Perhaps you and your partner are managing to stay in
school until you graduate even though you have a child.
Maybe that child is already out of the infant stage, and you
wonder if it might be nice to have another baby. Here are
some things to think about before you have intercourse
without using birth control:

• Most important, you want to give your first child the
care he needs. Toddlers need lots of attention.

• Finding outside care for two children is harder than
finding it for one.

• Babies are expensive. Can you afford another one?

• Your next baby is less likely to be born healthy if your
pregnancies are too close together.

• Each child takes time and attention away from your
partner.

Kianna and Sarah are just eleven months apart. When I got pregnant the second time, I was very disappointed, and I had bad thoughts about everything.

Since we've had the baby, we've had sex only twice. That really changes it. It makes you scared. I get the Depo-Provera every three months.

Neither of us was in the mood for sex right after delivery. We were both scared, and we both realized we didn't have to have sex in our relationship.

Elaine, 19/Antonio, 17 (Kianna, 13 months; Sarah, 2 months)

Choosing to have a baby is a big decision. If you have sexual intercourse without using birth control, that's what you're doing. You're choosing to have a baby.

Plan now to plan your family. You, your partner, and your current and future children deserve some choices.

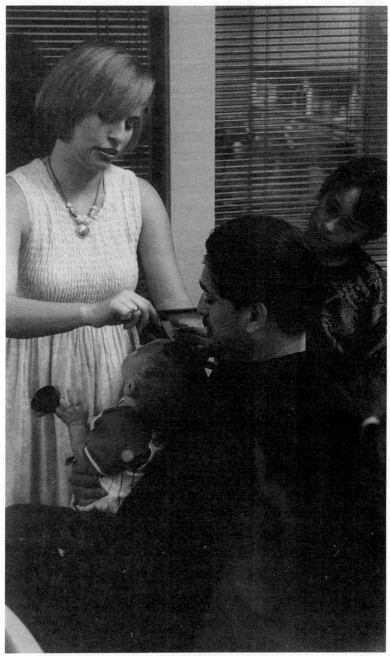

"We like to do family things."

CHAPTER 11

Donna and Tino — Ten Years Together

Donna and Tino, both now 25, have been living together for almost ten years. Their children are Tino, Jr., 9; Victoria, 7; and Emelio, 3 months.

Donna and Tino's relationship has not always run smoothly, but together they have developed a strong and caring life together. Their story illustrates many of the concepts in this book and in its companion volume, *Teenage Couples—Caring, Commitment and Change: How to Build a Relationship That Lasts*. It provides an upbeat approach to the challenges couples face as they share their lives.

Pregnancy—Family Isn't Happy

Tino: *We started living together during Donna's first pregnancy in 1984. She was 15, just before her*

16th birthday. We'd already been together two years.

Donna: *We moved in together because we found out I was pregnant. In my family, being the youngest and the only girl, my parents were not happy. They actually wanted me to get an abortion, but I didn't want to do that so I moved out. We asked Tino's parents if I could move in with them, and they said, "Sure." That's how we got started—with their help. We lived there about 2 years until we graduated from high school. I went to trade school to become a hair stylist and Tino started working.*

Tino was with me during pregnancy and childbirth. That was important.

Living with In-Laws

Tino: *That's what helped out—having my parents there until we started going where we wanted. It was hard having two families in the household. That was kind of rough, especially with my parents telling us how to raise our kid while we wanted to do it our way. Me and Donna had to do a lot of talking ourselves and not really argue with what was happening—this is just a part-time thing, and then we'll be out of here.*

Donna: *You have to keep thinking this is just a temporary thing. We believed in different ways of discipline. We were more liberal, and that's where arguments would spark up. We lived in one small house, two families, and arguments do come up.*

We would talk with them and explain, "This is our son, and this is the way we want to raise him. You brought up your children, and they are just fine. We need to experience raising our own children. We need to learn our own way."

We couldn't be doing it their way the rest of our lives because one day we'd be moving on. We'd have to do it ourselves.

Tino: *I'm the oldest son, and I wanted our son raised differently. I saw them doing the same kinds of things they had done with me, and I didn't want that. I didn't want that strictness.*

My parents didn't want me to play with kids in the neighborhood, and they never wanted to allow Tino, Jr. in the front yard to play. They were afraid something would happen to him. I would say, "You let him do that. He needs to do that. Let him get out there and experience a little bit." My mom is kind of hovering.

There were times when me and Donna had to sit in our room and just talk and keep our two worlds separated.

In a lot of families, especially in the Hispanic culture, the aunts and uncles want to be involved. Me and Donna would talk, "That's their lives, and if that's the way they see things, we have to separate ourselves from them." I think that helped a little. My cousin just recently divorced because of the meddling in the family.

Education Is a Must

Donna: *Another thing—a lot of Tino's cousins had teenage pregnancy, too, and they wouldn't let their wives go on to school. They insisted they stay home and take care of the kids.*

David (school counselor) *opened our eyes to the fact that in order to get on in the world, you have to finish your education. He showed us how we could raise our child, finish our education, and get a good start in life even though we were young and had a child. A lot of people think you can't do anything with a child, but your kids are really along for the ride.*

Once we finished high school, Tino went to work. I went on to Beauty College to become a hair stylist. We continued to live at his family's house.

Tino: *Soon after I went to work, we moved out. We had agreed that Donna would get her education and get her career started. Then I went back to college. I said, "It's my turn now."*

Donna: *I've been a hair stylist for eight years now.*

Setting Career Goals

Tino: *We're managing to get by with one income now, but once I'm done, we'll do better. I'm heading toward law enforcement. I have two more semesters of college and I'll have my AA degree. Then I'll go on to cadet training.*

That's a big thing, too. Me and Donna sat down before, when we were younger, and set our goals.

Donna: *It's important to set goals because if you don't, the days just go by.*

Tino: *Especially with the children, somebody has to work, somebody has to bring income in. I had a job while she was in school. Then when I was laid off, I decided it was time for me. This is my year.*

Donna: *We have always worked it out so when I was working or he was working, that our schedules were opposite one another. We never had to pay for daycare. Like right now I work and he goes to school during the hours I don't work. Somebody is always home with the baby.*

Tino: *And there's a lot more bonding with the children doing it this way. They have little chores they have to do now, 9 and 7. They have responsibilities,* *and it creates more of a family atmosphere. We're always doing things together. Both of our kids are doing well.*

The Marriage Decision

Donna: *Shortly after our daughter was born, we moved out, and later that year we got married. We decided we were really in this together. We waited that long because we wanted to make sure this is what we wanted. So often teenagers who are pregnant get married just because they're pregnant or their parents force them to. We married because we wanted to.*

Tino: *It wasn't a marriage out of convenience. And a lot of teenagers today want to escape their family. They think they will be able to go somewhere else and plant their roots, but it doesn't work that way. There's a lot more to having a child than they think. It's really a lifetime commitment.*

Donna: *Sure, the ideal way would be for people to fall in love, get married, and have a baby, but it doesn't always work like that. I guess if they know and believe they can work things out, and it's a give and take relationship . . .*

Tino: *There has to be give and take, just sitting there and talking and discussing, and not have it through anger. Discuss your goals, know what's going on. I think that's what has helped me and Donna — we have always talked and really let each other know what we're doing.*

Jealousy—A Little

Donna: *Both of us have a little bit of jealousy.*
Tino: *But we don't let it get the better of us.*

Donna: *I'd say maybe when we were young teen-agers, first together, I think then we both had a harder time with jealousy. It didn't matter if we spoke with another woman or another man. That wouldn't make us jealous, but if that person made comments about your spouse . . . his sister was jealous of me moving into their home. She thought I was taking her place, and her parents gave me a lot of attention because I was pregnant.*

I'd say Tino was more jealous until the last five years. I think over the years the trust builds, showing him I'm not going to be out fooling around with anybody else. I'm faithful to him. And where would I find time to be with anybody else?

Tino: *Another thing my relatives didn't like was that it was okay with me for Donna to go out of town. Because of the business she's in, she has to go to shows in other states. My relatives are totally against it. "But why?" I would say. "That's her job, that's what she needs to do." They can't even trust their wives around anybody else.*

Once I went to my cousin's house to deliver an invitation to my son's birthday party, and she wouldn't unlock the door. They didn't come, and I heard they got in a big old argument because I had been over there. When we are around them, all the wives have to look down. They get upset with Donna because she is real outspoken.

Donna: *When I became pregnant, my family didn't speak to me until just before Tino, Jr., was born. Then they started coming around and wanting to see me and the baby.*

It's totally different now. As I was growing up, we were not a real close family. Now I feel closer than I did then. They always want us to come for dinner.

*When we moved into our new house a year ago, we
didn't have a washer and dryer, and they got us one.*

What About Hitting?

Donna: *I'd say if that happens to somebody, they
have got to seek counseling or get out of the relationship. We had one incident like that a long time before
our oldest was born. I spoke with David about it at
school. David talked with Tino and explained to him
that's not the way you treat a woman.*

*I also told Tino that couldn't happen again. You
have to give yourself a limit as to what you'll take. I
think with counseling . . . us being real close with
David makes it easy to talk to somebody.*

Communication Tips

Donna: *I think communication has gotten better
through the years. In the beginning we started out as
friends and that helps. Him being my best friend
through high school — and you share everything with
your best friend. Over the years you get to really
know the person, what they will do, how they will
react, and you learn to communicate a lot better.*

*We learned we have to express ourselves and let
each other know what we're doing.*

Tino: *You can't keep it all bottled up inside. You
can't do that. Maybe a mentor can help, somebody
outside your family. They can also give you advice on
how to go about doing things. Somebody positive.*

Sharing the Work and the Joy

Donna: *We share household tasks.*
Tino: *My family is so much into the male domi-
nance thing. They think we're strange.*

Donna: *We're kind of backward on this, and his family thinks we're crazy. My husband does all the cooking. He's good at it and he likes to cook. The cleaning—it gets done. One or the other does it. Tino doesn't have a problem with doing laundry or vacuuming.*

Tino: *I was the oldest, and my parents left me at home to watch my brothers and sisters. I was the father figure to them. I watched them, I made dinner, and I washed clothes. I always wanted to help my mom out because she would come home from work and be tired.*

Donna: *I don't mind cooking, but it's one less thing I have to do. Taking care of the children is pretty shared, too. I breastfeed the new baby so the feeding comes from me.*

I pump and Tino has to warm up the milk. I found a very light weight and portable breast pump that works well for $150. It only weighs about two pounds and comes in a little tote bag. It's real nice. I pump at work. It also comes with thermal bags and ice bags.

Tino: *We figure Donna breastfeeding Emelio will save us at least $1,000 the first year because we don't have to buy formula. And it's better for the baby.*

Donna: *Tino has always been supportive of me breastfeeding the kids. When he comes back from school, he takes the baby so I can rest before I go to work.*

Tino: *I'm the one who sends the older two kids to school.*

Learning to Handle Money

Donna: *We have learned always to live on a budget. We made the mistake when we were younger,*

Donna and Tino plan their work and school schedules
so one can always be home with Emelio.

*when we first moved out together. We bought a car.
We got credit cards. Then we got behind on our credit
card, and we let ourselves get drowned. We had to get
a loan from the bank to pay off that credit card. So
we've never had a credit card since. Now we probably need to get one for business purposes. We have
pretty much learned, but it's hard always to budget
ourselves.*

Tino: *And we don't do like some people do. We
don't say, "That's your money and this is my money."
We put the money in a pile, and pay our bills. Then
we divide whatever is left over. It's not like this is*

*your money for the rent and mine will pay the
telephone. Instead ours is one pot.*

Donna: *I think money causes a lot of arguments.
People say that's my money, and you can't spend my
money. I do balance our checkbook, but it has both
our names on it.*

Tino: *That wasn't always the case. One time I tried
writing a check for groceries and they didn't allow
me to write it because it just said "Donna Delgadillo"
on the account. We agreed that didn't make sense, so
we changed it.*

The Diaper Question

Donna: *We use cloth diapers, and we have a
diaper service. The main issue is the environmental.
I used cloth with the other two children, too. In
addition to being expensive, disposables are a real
problem for the environment.*

Tino: *Diaper service is convenient too. You have a
stack there, and by the end of the week it's replaced.
You don't have to wash them out or anything, just bag
them in a container 'til next week. It's lots easier.*

Donna: *And you don't have to worry about running out. We pay $43/month for diaper service.*

Tino: *One of Donna's girlfriends calls her the
natural mother, like cloth diapers, breastfeeding.*

Disciplining Together

Donna: *I don't believe in spanking while Tino
does if it gets to an extreme. But if he uses just a stern
voice, they will do it right away or be in tears.*

Tino: *We did have a disagreement in the beginning
about spanking. I was spanked, and I thought it was*

*the way to go. So we had our disagreements. Then
I found other ways that worked better. With my son,
calling him by his full name upsets him more than the
spanking.*

Donna: *Because Tino was more the disciplinarian
and myself not, I would say, "Oh don't be too rough"
and I would overlook it or I'd baby them. Now that
my son is 9, he doesn't mind me as well. I get more
back talk with him. That could be because I babied
him too much.*

Tino: *She used to call me at work and say, "Tino,
little Tino, Jr. is acting up here at the house. Why
don't you talk to him?" She'd hand the phone to him,
and I'd tell him to go to his room. Then I figured how
this made me the bad guy and I wasn't even there. So
I told her to take care of it, and I'd love him up, too.*

Donna: *By the time the second came along, Tino
became less stern, and I tried to be more stern. That
made it more equal, and that's probably why Victoria
is real well-behaved.*

Tino: *Talking works better than spanking. Your
child learns better when you discuss the problems
with him.*

Donna: *They went through a stage of saying bad
words. We would say "Do you know what that
means?"*

"No."

*"Well, you shouldn't say it unless you know what it
means."*

Tino: *When one of the kids gets to an age, he has
to do certain things. Then when the next one is this
age, she has to do it. I try to keep an age limit on
what they're doing, try to keep everything as equal as
possible for their ages.*

Keeping the Romance Alive

Donna: *We do a lot of things together. We like to do family things. We like to go to the movies as a family, go to the park.*

Tino: *Vacationing—like our honeymoon. Our honeymoon was a family vacation. We all got in the car and went to San Diego to the Zoo, Wild Animal Park, Disneyland.*

Donna: *Most of the time we do things together, but he has his friends and I have my friends. He doesn't like to shop, so I go shopping with my girlfriends. I go to hair shows. He and his dad like to work on cars and go to car shows. I go to hair shows a lot out of town, with co-workers. He doesn't mind because he can do things men do.*

After having the children, my sexual drive has gone down.

Tino: *Mine hasn't.*

Donna: *Doing other things together, like going out to dinner and dancing helps keep the sex alive.*

Tino: *We went to that bed and breakfast inn. She surprised me with that on our fifth anniversary.*

Donna: *I went to the salon, put on my wedding gown, got my hair done, and put on the make-up. I got his suit out, and went over to where he was painting a house. I got out of the car with my wedding dress on, and said, "Hurry and change your clothes." And I surprised him with a night at the B&B.*

Tino: *Just doing something by yourselves helps keep the romance alive.*

*A lot of young people have to realize the grass is **not** greener on the other side. As long as you keep your own relationship watered and nurtured, it will be just as green—or even greener.*

Donna: *Maybe they see somebody they think is better, then they get a divorce, then they realize the next one is not better. It's easier if you just work out your relationship rather than giving up and quitting.*

Tino: *Nothing comes easy. If you really want to make it work, you have to work at it.*

Donna: *If you have people to support you and help you out. We had that at Daylor High School. And living with my in-laws who had been teenaged and pregnant, and they could remember what it was like. We got a lot of support from them. We were lucky to have support.*

Tino and Donna illustrate important factors for building a satisfying forever relationship. He was there from the time they took the prenatal health and parenting classes at Daylor High School through today as they each pursue their careers and parent three children together. Each is there for the other. They support each other, and in the process, continue to build their relationship together.

I hope you and your partner can be as caring toward each other. May your love and your relationship be forever!

APPENDIX

Description of Interviewees

Sometimes a problem becomes easier to deal with if you know you aren't the only one with such a problem. Hearing someone else talk about feelings of jealousy, for example, may help you look more realistically at your own situation.

This book and its companion title, *Teenage Couples— Caring, Commitment and Change: How to Build a Relationship that Lasts,* are based on information, opinions, and suggestions from 80 young people I interviewed extensively. Each was living or had lived with a partner.

Thirty-one of the interviewees were married, and for 13 couples, both husband and wife were interviewed.

Of the 31 married interviewees, 18 did not live together before they were married while 13 did.

Twelve of the interviewees were no longer living with their partner, although three were still "together."

Sixty-five of the 80 interviewees had lived together with his parents or hers. Half of the total group were still with parents at the time of the interview, while 40 were living by themselves at that time.

Almost half of the interviewees (39) were living in California. Other states represented by interviewees included Florida, Georgia, Pennsylvania, Ohio, Illinois, Nebraska, Montana, and Oregon.

Interviewee Data

Sex	Male		Female				
	26		54				

Age	14	15	16	17	18	19	20	21+
	1	3	11	19	19	8	7	12

Note: All were living with a partner before age 20 or, if older, lived with a partner younger than 20.

Lived together	≤1 yr.	1-2 yr.	2-3 yr.	3+ yr.
	25	36	12	7

Married?	Yes	No		
	29	51		

Ethnic Group	Hispanic	White	Black	Native Am	Asian
	28	30	12	7	3

Number of Children	None	Pregnant	1	2	3
	4	7	58	10	1

Marriage Expectations Questionnaire

The Marriage Expectations Survey included a number of descriptive questions, questions designed to provide information about the survey group. Most of the questions, however, dealt directly with attitudes toward marriage and living together.

You might find that answering and discussing the following 76 questions with your partner would help each of you understand better how the other feels about various issues. It would be best for each of you to answer all of the questions alone, then share your answers. The results may surprise you both.

Permission is granted to make copies of the questionnaire in order to make it easier to use. If you copy it, simply circle on your copy the letter of the answer of your choice. Otherwise, you and your partner can each number 1-76 on

a sheet of paper, then write the letter of your chosen answer
next to the appropriate number.

Remember—discussing your answers together may help
you understand each other more completely.

1. How do you feel about a young couple living with either his
   or her parents?

   A. Good idea   **B.** Okay until we save some money
   C. I'd rather not   **D.** I'm totally against it

2. If you have a problem, to whom are you most likely to talk?

   A. Nobody   **B.** Parents
   C. Boy/girl friend (or husband/wife)   **D.** Another friend
   E. Teacher   **F.** Counselor   **G.** Minister   **H.** Other

3. When you and your partner have an argument, how do you
   settle it? (More than one answer is okay.)

   A. Quit talking to each other   **B.** Yell
   C. Talk it through together   **D.** Talk to my parents or hers
   E. Talk to someone else   **F.** Slug it out
   G. Get a referee   **H.** We do not argue

4. When/if you marry, would you like your marriage to be much
   like your parents' marriage?

   A. Absolutely   **B.** Probably
   C. Probably not   **D.** Absolutely not

5. When you get married, do you expect it to last the rest of
   your life?

   A. Absolutely   **B.** Probably
   C. Probably not   **D.** Absolutely not

6. Would you prefer to marry a person from your own ethnic
   group or race?

   A. Absolutely   **B.** Probably
   C. Probably not   **D.** Absolutely not

7. Do you think marrying a person from a different ethnic group
   would cause problems for you?

   A. Absolutely   **B.** Probably
   C. Probably not   **D.** Absolutely not

8. Would you prefer to marry a person who has the same religious beliefs as you do?

    A. Absolutely   **B.** Probably

    C. Probably not   **D.** Absolutely not

9. Do you think marrying a person with different religious beliefs would cause problems for you?

    A. Absolutely   **B.** Probably

    C. Probably not   **D.** Absolutely not

10. Is it all right for a couple to have sexual intercourse before they marry?

    A. Absolutely   **B.** Probably

    C. Probably not   **D.** Absolutely not

11. How do you feel about a man and woman living together if they aren't married?

    A. It's okay   **B.** It's okay *if* they plan to marry later

    C. It's okay but I wouldn't do it   **D.** I think it's wrong

12. When a teenage girl gets pregnant, should she and her boyfriend get married?

    A. Absolutely   **B.** Probably   **C.** It depends on their situation

    D. Probably not   **E.** Absolutely not

13. If a man gets a woman pregnant, should he take responsibility for the pregnancy and the child?

    A. Absolutely   **B.** Probably

    C. Probably not   **D.** Absolutely not

14. Do you think it's important for a child to live with both of his parents?

    A. Absolutely   **B.** Probably

    C. Probably not   **D.** Absolutely not

15. If you had a child, what effect do you think she'd have on your relationship with her other parent?

    A. Very good   **B.** Somewhat good

    C. No effect   **D.** Somewhat bad   **E.** Very bad

16. How do you feel about a man hitting his partner?
    A. It should never happen
    B. It's not good, but sometimes it's necessary
    C. It's not okay, but it may happen when he's angry or drunk
    D. It's okay

17. How do you feel about a woman hitting her partner?
    A. It should never happen
    B. It's not good, but sometimes it's necessary
    C. It's not okay, but it may happen when he's angry or drunk
    D. It's okay

18. Has a date or your partner ever hit you?
    A. Never   **B.** Once   **C.** Two times
    D. Three times   **E.** Four times   **F.** Five or more

19. Have you ever hit a date or your partner?
    A. Never   **B.** Once   **C.** Two times
    D. Three times   **E.** Four times   **F.** Five or more

How much do you think getting married or living with a partner at age 18 or younger would change your life in the following areas?

20. Money: **A.** I'd have more money
    B. It would make no difference   **C.** I'd have less money

21. Friends: **A.** More friends **B.** Fewer friends
    C. Different friends   **D.** No change

22. Recreation/Partying:
    A. More   **B.** No change   **C.** Less recreation/partying

23. Free Time:
    A. More   **B.** No change   **C.** Less free time

24. Relationship with your family:
    A. Closer   **B.** No change   **C.** Less close

25. School attendance:
   A. Attendance would improve
   B. No change
   C. Attendance would drop
   D. I would drop out of school

26. College/Trade school:
   A. I'd be more likely to attend
   B. No change
   C. Less likely to attend

27. If you married or moved in with a partner before you graduated from high school, would you want your partner to continue his/her education?
   A. Absolutely
   B. Probably
   C. It doesn't matter
   D. Probably not
   E. Absolutely not

28. For your relationship to be successful, would you and your partner need to have enough money for your important needs?
   A. Absolutely
   B. Probably
   C. It doesn't matter
   D. Probably not
   E. Absolutely not

29. Should married or living-together partners agree on how they spend money?
   A. Absolutely
   B. Probably
   C. It doesn't matter
   D. Probably not
   E. Absolutely not

30. In a *good* marriage, should the husband earn most of the money?
   A. Absolutely
   B. Probably
   C. It doesn't matter
   D. Probably not
   E. Absolutely not

31. In a *good* marriage, should the wife do most of the cooking and housekeeping?
   A. Absolutely
   B. Probably
   C. It doesn't matter
   D. Probably not
   E. Absolutely not

32. Do you think it is important for a mother and father to agree on how to discipline their children?
   A. Absolutely
   B. Probably
   C. It doesn't matter
   D. Probably not
   E. Absolutely not

If/when you marry or live with a partner, who do you feel should be responsible for the following tasks?

33. Earning money: **A.** Woman only   **B.** Woman mostly
    C. Both   **D.** Man mostly   **E.** Man only

34. Deciding how money is spent:
    A. Woman only   **B.** Woman mostly   **C.** Both
    D. Man mostly   **E.** Man only

35. Paying bills: **A.** Woman only   **B.** Woman mostly
    C. Both   **D.** Man mostly   **E.** Man only

36. Vacuuming the house:
    A. Woman only   **B.** Woman mostly   **C.** Both
    D. Man mostly   **E.** Man only

37. Mopping floors: **A.** Woman only   **B.** Woman mostly
    C. Both   **D.** Man mostly   **E.** Man only

38. Preparing meals: **A.** Woman only   **B.** Woman mostly
    C. Both   **D.** Man mostly   **E.** Man only

39. Cleaning up after meals:
    A. Woman only   **B.** Woman mostly   **C.** Both
    D. Man mostly   **E.** Man only

40. Doing family laundry:
    A. Woman only   **B.** Woman mostly   **C.** Both
    D. Man mostly   **E.** Man only

41. Washing the car:
    A. Woman only   **B.** Woman mostly   **C.** Both
    D. Man mostly   **E.** Man only

42. Mowing the lawn:
    A. Woman only   **B.** Woman mostly   **C.** Both
    D. Man mostly   **E.** Man only

43. Changing baby's diapers:
    A. Woman only   **B.** Woman mostly   **C.** Both
    D. Man mostly   **E.** Man only

44. Feeding babies and children:
   A. Woman only   **B.** Woman mostly   **C.** Both
   D. Man mostly   **E.** Man only

45. Bathing baby: **A.** Woman only   **B.** Woman mostly
   C. Both   **D.** Man mostly   **E.** Man only

46. Putting baby to bed:
   A. Woman only   **B.** Woman mostly   **C.** Both
   D. Man mostly   **E.** Man only

47. Putting toddler to bed:
   A. Woman only   **B.** Woman mostly   **C.** Both
   D. Man mostly   **E.** Man only

48. Disciplining children:
   A. Woman only   **B.** Woman mostly   **C.** Both
   D. Man mostly   **E.** Man only

49. Playing with the children:
   A. Woman only   **B.** Woman mostly   **C.** Both
   D. Man mostly   **E.** Man only

How important is it that the person you marry or live with have the following qualities?

50. Good money manager:
   A. Very important   **B.** Somewhat important
   C. Not important

51. Loves and cares about children:
   A. Very important   **B.** Somewhat important
   C. Not important

52. Good cook:
   A. Very important   **B.** Somewhat important
   C. Not important

53. Good housekeeper:
   A. Very important   **B.** Somewhat important
   C. Not important

54. Knows how to make plumbing and other home repairs:
    A. Very important   B. Somewhat important
    C. Not important

55. Takes care of the yard:
    A. Very important   B. Somewhat important
    C. Not important

56. Good sex partner:
    A. Very important   B. Somewhat important
    C. Not important

57. Shares common interests with you:
    A. Very important   B. Somewhat important
    C. Not important

58. Spends most of his/her time with you:
    A. Very important   B. Somewhat important
    C. Not important

59. Do you expect to work outside your home if you have no children?
    A. Yes   B. Probably   C. Probably not   D. Absolutely not

60. Do you expect your partner to work outside your home if you have no children?
    A. Yes   B. Probably   C. Probably not   D. Absolutely not

61. Do you expect to work outside your home if you have children under two years of age?
    A. Yes   B. Probably   C. Probably not   D. Absolutely not

62. Do you expect your partner to work outside your home if you have children under two years of age?
    A. Yes   B. Probably   C. Probably not   D. Absolutely not

63. Do you expect to work outside your home if you have children aged two to five?
    A. Yes   B. Probably   C. Probably not   D. Absolutely not

64. Do you expect your partner to work outside your home if you have children aged two to five?
    A. Yes   B. Probably   C. Probably not   D. Absolutely not

65. Do you expect to work outside your home if all your children are in school?

   A. Yes   **B.** Probably   **C.** Probably not   **D.** Absolutely not

66. Do you expect your partner to work outside your home if all your children are in school?

   A. Yes   **B.** Probably   **C.** Probably not   **D.** Absolutely not

67. Would it be all right with you if the woman in your partnership earned more money than the man?

   A. Yes   **B.** Probably   **C.** Probably not   **D.** Absolutely not

68. Is it all right for a man to tell his partner that she must *not* work away from home?

   A. Yes   **B.** Probably   **C.** Probably not   **D.** Absolutely not

69. Is it all right for a man to tell his partner that she *must* work away from home?

   A. Yes   **B.** Probably   **C.** Probably not   **D.** Absolutely not

70. Is it all right for a man to stay home while his partner gets a job?

   A. Yes   **B.** Probably   **C.** Probably not   **D.** Absolutely not

71. **MALES:** Would you be jealous if your girlfriend or wife looked at other boys?

   FEMALES: Would you be jealous if your boyfriend or husband looked at other girls?

   A. Absolutely   **B.** Probably
   C. Probably not   **D.** Absolutely not

72. **MALES:** Would you be jealous if your girlfriend or wife talked with other boys?

   FEMALES: Would you be jealous if your boyfriend or husband talked with other girls?

   A. Absolutely   **B.** Probably
   C. Probably not   **D.** Absolutely not

73. **MALES:** Would you be jealous if your girlfriend or wife worked with other boys?

   FEMALES: Would you be jealous if your boyfriend or husband worked with other girls?

A. Absolutely	**B.** Probably
C. Probably not	**D.** Absolutely not

74. **MALES:** Would you be jealous if your girlfriend or wife went to school with other boys?

   FEMALES: Would you be jealous if your boyfriend or husband went to school with other girls?

A. Absolutely	**B.** Probably
C. Probably not	**D.** Absolutely not

75. **MALES:** Would you be jealous if your girlfriend or wife went to a concert with another boy?

   FEMALES: Would you be jealous if your boyfriend or husband went to a concert with another girl?

A. Absolutely	**B.** Probably
C. Probably not	**D.** Absolutely not

76. **MALES:** Would you be jealous if your girlfriend or wife had a close male friend?

   FEMALES: Would you be jealous if your boyfriend or husband had a close female friend?

A. Absolutely	**B.** Probably
C. Probably not	**D.** Absolutely not

ANNOTATED BIBLIOGRAPHY

Many books are available in which marriage in general is discussed. Several hundred titles are listed under "Marriage" in the current edition of *Books in Print.* Quite a few resources concerned with teenage pregnancy and parenthood have been published. However, there are very few books dealing directly with teenage marriage. In fact, the same edition of *Books in Print* lists only two under "Teenage Marriage."

The following bibliography includes the books mentioned in *Teenage Couples: Coping with Reality.* Also listed are some especially good titles for and about pregnant adolescents and school-age parents. A few novels with this theme are included. Easy readability, high interest level, and practicality of information were the major criteria for selection of titles.

Price quotes are from *Books in Print,* 1994. Because prices change so rapidly, however, and because publishers move, it is wise to call your local library reference department for an updated price and address before ordering a book. If you can't find a book you want in your bookstore, you can usually get it directly from the publisher. Enclose $2.50 for shipping in addition to the price of the book. See page 192 for an order form for Morning Glory Press publications.

Adams, Pat, and Marc Jacobs. *Yo! Let's Eat!!* 1994. 96 pp. $7.95 + $5
shpg. The National Resource Center for Youth Services, 202 West
Eighth Street, Tulsa, OK 74119. 918/585-2986.
*A wonderful cookbook of easy-to-fix favorite recipes from teenagers. The
"Easy Dinners" section is probably the most helpful for people who haven't
cooked much.*

Arthur, Shirley. *Surviving Teen Pregnancy: Your Choices, Dreams
and Decisions.* 1991. 192 pp. Paper, $9.95. Teacher's Guide and
Study Guide, $2.50 set. Quantity discount. Morning Glory Press,
6595 San Haroldo Way, Buena Park, CA 90620. 714/828-1998.
*Helps pregnant teens understand their alternatives. Offers guidance in
learning decision-making. Most important, it can help readers regain
control of their lives and get on with their plans and their dreams.*

Brazelton, T. Barry. *Toddlers and Parents: A Declaration of
Independence.* 1989. 249 pp. $16.00. Doubleday and Co., Inc.,
1540 Broadway, New York, NY 10036-4094. 800/223-6834.
*Brazelton's discussions of parenting are hard to beat. Beautiful photos. See
his other books about babies and families, too.*

Brinkley, Ginny, and Sherry Sampson. Illus. by Gail Spratt Cooper.
You and Your New Baby: A Book for Young Mothers. Also in
Spanish—*Usted y su nuevo bebe.* 1991. 80 pp. $4.95. Quantity
discounts. Pink Inc! P.O. Box 866, Atlantic Beach, FL 32233-0866.
904/285-9276.
*Simple and complete guide for caring for baby. Written in a format for easy
understanding.*

_____. *Young and Pregnant—A Book For You.* Also in Spanish:
Joven y embarazada. 1989. 73 pp. $4.95. Pink Inc!
*Refreshingly simple book on prenatal care directed to teenagers. Provides
basic information.*

Eley, Eleanor. **"You and Your Baby: Playing and Learning To-
gether." "You and Your Baby: A Special Relationship."** 1994. 32
pp. each. $2.65 each. Bulk discounts. The Corner Health Center, 47
North Huron Street, Ypsilanti, MI 48197. 313/484-3700.
*Gorgeous photos of teen parents and their children on every other page.
Simple but very helpful copy.*

Heine, Arthur J. *Surviving After High School: Overcoming Life's
Hurdles.* 1991. 244 pp. $18 ppd. J-Mart Press. Order from Keller-

Huff Training and Consulting, R.R. 2, Box 276, Highway 100, Hermann, MO 65041. 314/486-5348.
Contains an amazing amount of quite-readable information about independent living—getting and keeping a job, taxes, budgets, shopping, handling a checking account and credit card, housing, transportation, and much more. Excellent information source for teens highly motivated to live on their own and make it work.

Leach, Penelope. *Your Baby and Child from Birth to Age Five.*
Revised, 1989. 554 pp. Hardcover, $19.95; paper, $16.95. Alfred A. Knopf, 400 Hahn Road, Westminster, MD 21157. 800/733-3000.
An absolutely beautiful book packed with information, many color photos and lovely drawings. Comprehensive, authoritative, and outstandingly sensitive guide to child care and development.

Lindsay, Jeanne Warren. *Do I Have a Daddy? A Story About a Single-Parent Child.* 1991. 48 pp. Paper, $5.95; hardcover, $12.95. Free study guide. Morning Glory Press, 6595 San Haroldo Way, Buena Park, CA 90620. 714/828-1998.
A beautiful book for the child who has never met his/her father. A special sixteen-page section offers suggestions to single mothers.

_____. *School-Age Parents: The Challenge of Three-Generation Living.* 1990. 224 pp. Paper, $10.95; hardcover, $17.95. Teacher's Guide/Study Guide, $2.50 set. Morning Glory Press.
A much needed book for dealing with the frustrations, problems, and pleasures of three-generation living. Useful for helping teen parents communicate with their parents.

_____. *Teen Dads: Rights, Responsibilities and Joys.* 1993. 192 pp. Paper, $9.95; hardcover, $15.95. Teacher's Guide and Workbook, $2.50 each. Morning Glory Press.
A how-to-parent book especially for teenage fathers. Offers help in parenting from conception to age 3 of the child. Many quotes from and photos of teen fathers.

_____. *Teenage Couples—Caring, Commitment and Change: How to Build a Lasting Relationship.* 1995. 208 pp. Paper, $9.95; hardcover, $15.95. Study Guide, $2.50. Curriculum Guide (also includes *Teenage Couples—Coping with Reality*), $19.95. Morning Glory Press.
Covers such important topics as communication, handling arguments, keeping romance alive, sex in a relationship, jealousy, alcohol and drug addiction, partner abuse, and divorce. Lots of quotes from teenage couples.

_____. *Teens Parenting—The Challenge of Toddlers*. 1991. 192
pp. Paper, $9.95; hardcover, $15.95. Workbook, $2.50. Morning
Glory Press.
*How-to-parent book especially for teenage parents of toddlers. It's the
follow-up book to Teens Parenting—Your Baby's First Year. Lots more
quotes from teenage parents who share their experiences and their
parenting techniques.*

_____. *Teens Parenting—Your Baby's First Year*. 1991. 192 pp.
Paper, $9.95; hardcover, $15.95. Workbook, $2.50. Morning Glory
Press.
*A how-to-parent book for teen parents during that all-important first year of
parenthood. Many quotes from teen parents illustrate the concepts
discussed.*

_____, and Jean Brunelli. *Teens Parenting—Your Pregnancy and
Newborn Journey*. 1991. 192 pp. Spanish edition, *Adolescentes
como padres—Jornada de tu embarazo y nacimiento del bebe*.
1993. Paper, $9.95; hardcover, $15.95. Workbook for each edition,
$2.50. Teacher's guide for Spanish edition, $2.50. Morning Glory
Press.
*Prenatal health book for pregnant teenagers. Includes section on care of the
newborn and a chapter for fathers. Also available in Easier Reading Edition
(third grade reading level) with workbook and teacher's guide. Same prices
as above.*

_____ and Sally McCullough. *Teens Parenting—Discipline from
Birth to Three*. 1991. 192 pp. Paper, $9.95; hardcover, $15.95.
Workbook, $2.50. Discounts on sets of four *Teens Parenting* books
and on sets of workbooks. Morning Glory Press.
*Provides teenage parents with guidelines to help prevent discipline
problems with their children and guidelines for dealing with problems when
they occur.*

MELD Parenting Materials. Nueva Familia: Six books in Spanish and
English. *Baby Is Here. Feeding Your Child, 5 months-2 years.
Healthy Child, Sick Child. Safe Child and Emergencies. Baby
Grows. Baby Plays*. 1992. $9 each. MELD, Suite 507, 123 North
Third Street, Minneapolis, MN 55401. 612/332-7563.
*Very easy to read books full of information. Designed especially for
Mexican and Mexican American families, but excellent for anyone with
limited reading skills. Ask MELD for catalog of other materials designed
especially for school-age parents.*

Parent Express Series: *Parent Express: For You and Your Infant.*
Spanish edition: Noticlas para los padres. *Parent Express: For You
and Your Toddler.* Each newsletter, 8 pp. $3.50 each set. ANR
Publications, University of California, 6701 San Pablo Avenue,
Oakland, CA 94608-1239. 510/642-2431.
Wonderful series of newsletters for parents. The first set, available in
English and Spanish, starts two months before delivery and continues
monthly through the first year of the child's life. Second set with twelve
letters covers second and third years. Good resource for teen parents.
Beautiful photos, easy reading.

Reynolds, Marilyn. *Detour for Emmy.* 1993. 256 pp. Paper, $8.95;
hardcover, $15.95. Quantity discounts. Free study guide on request.
Morning Glory Press, 6595 San Haroldo Way, Buena Park, CA
90620. 714/828-1998.
Fascinating fiction—the story of Emmy through first love to handling her
unanticipated pregnancy alone to parenting her child—and working toward
her new goals in her life as a young mother alone. Author works with
school-age parents, and her writing shows a special understanding of
their world.

_____. *Too Soon for Jeff.* 1994. 224 pp. Paper, $8.95; hardcover,
$15.95. Free study guide on request. Morning Glory Press.
Another wonderful novel. Jeff is a reluctant teenage father who thought his
girlfriend was on the pill. She "forgot to take it sometimes," and now she's
pregnant. Jeff first denies his parenthood, then accepts the many changes
in his life.

Schneider, Phyllis. *Parents Book of Infant Colic.* 1990. 168 pp. $3.95.
Ballantine Books, 400 Hahn Road, Westminster, MD 21157.
301/848-1900.
Anyone with a colicky baby will find this little book helpful. It's an in-depth
discussion of the subject with suggestions for helping parents and babies.

Wilkes, Donald L., and Viola Hamilton-Wilkes. *Teen Guide—Job*
Search: 10 Easy Steps to Your Future. 1993. 112 pp. $10. JEM/
JOB Educational Materials, 1230 East Main Street, Alhambra, CA
91801. 818/308-7642.
Easy reading, lots of illustrations. Simplified, practical, basic approach to
job hunting. Excellent for teens beginning their job search—and for those
teens who, because of lack of basic skills and/or lack of employed family
role models, show little interest in getting a job. Good resource.

ABOUT THE AUTHOR

Jeanne Warren Lindsay has worked with hundreds of pregnant and parenting teenagers. She developed the Teen Parent Program at Tracy

High School, Cerritos, California, in 1972, and coordinated the program for many years. She is the author of 15 other books dealing with adolescent pregnancy and parenting. Her *Teens Parenting* four-book series and *Teen Dads: Rights, Responsibilities and Joys* are widely used with pregnant and parenting teens.

Jeanne has graduate degrees in Anthropology and Home Economics. She and Bob have five children and five grandchildren.

ABOUT THE PHOTOGRAPHER

David Crawford, M.A., has been a photographer and counselor to pregnant and parenting teens for more than 25 years in the Elk Grove Unified School District, Sacra-

mento, California, where he co-directs the Program for Pregnant and Parenting Students. His quiet fatherly image has been a settling force in the personal lives of many of his students and their families. David teaches prenatal care, parenting, and photography, blending education and training to enhance his students' confidence and self-esteem.

David and Peggy have a son, Alton, 24, and have co-parented several other children. He is godfather to many others.

INDEX

Abstinence, 144-145
AFDC, 105-106
AIDS, 147, 149-150
Allowance, individual, 79-80, 96
Arguments, 116
Armed Forces, education benefits, 105
Baby expense, 83-86, 91
Baby food, 85
Birth control pill, 147
Birth control, talking about, 150
Breastfeeding, 148
Brunelli, Jean, 125-127
Budget, 26, 88-99
Carl Perkins Sex Equity Funding, 112
Checking account, 80-81
Child care, 104-105
Communication, 150, 161
Condoms, 145
Contraception, 142-153

Convenience foods, 95
Coupons, 86-87
Credit cards, 81-83, 163
Cultural differences, 42-43, 65-68
Delgadillo, Donna and Tino, 154-166
Depo-Provera, 125, 148
Discipline, 137-141, 157, 164-165
Disposable diapers, 83-85, 163-164
Education, 103-105, 157-158
Employment, 76, 79, 97-98, 100-112
Equal marriage, 52, 55, 57-59
Ethnic food preferences, 65-68
Extended family, 23, 30-45, 120-121, 156, 160
Family planning, 142-153
Fast foods, expense of, 64-65
Food Pyramid, 69-71
Food shopping, 72-73, 97

Goal setting, 112, 158-159
GRADS, 106
Grandparents, 140-141
Househusband, 55- 56
Housework, 33-36, 47-59
Housing, 26, 44
Implant, 147
Infant care, 131-137
IUD, 146
Jealousy, 159-160
Job Corps, 109-110
Job experience, 113
JTPA, 107
Marriage decision, 159
Marriage Expectations Survey,
    32, 55, 62, 106, 107-108
Meal planning, 68-73
Meal preparation, 60-69
Money problems, 19, 21, 27-28,
    50, 52, 102, 74-99
Mood swings of pregnancy, 116
Needs assessment evaluation, 112
Non-traditional jobs, 112
Nutrition, 69-71

Parenthood, 127, 128-141
Partner abuse, 161
Pregnancy, 114-127, 155-156
Pregnancy, father's role, 116-123
Prenatal care, 121-123
Prepared childbirth, 116
Privacy, lack of, 36-38
Roles, 47-59, 62, 161-162
School to Career Programs, 107
School to Work Opportunities
    Act, 107
Sexuality, 124-127
Siblings, 41-42
Smoking, effect on baby, 123-124
Spending record, 92-94
STD, 146, 149-150
Teen father stereotypes, 136
Three-generation living, 23,
    30-45, 120-121, 156
Time orientation, 99
Unemployment, 107-110
Welfare, 105-106
Wilson, Susan, 11-14
Work experience credit, 112

OTHER RESOURCES FROM MORNING GLORY PRESS

TEENAGE COUPLES—Caring, Commitment and Change: How to Build a Relationship that Lasts. TEENAGE COUPLES— Coping with Reality: Dealing with Money, In-Laws, Babies and Other Details of Daily Life. Two books to help teenage couples develop healthy, loving and lasting relationships.

TEENS PARENTING—Your Pregnancy and Newborn Journey How to take care of yourself and your newborn. For pregnant teens. Available in "regular" (RL 6), Easier Reading (RL 3), and Spanish.

TEENS PARENTING—Your Baby's First Year
TEENS PARENTING—The Challenge of Toddlers
TEENS PARENTING—Discipline from Birth to Three Three how-to-parent books especially for teenage parents.

VIDEO: "Discipline from Birth to Three" supplements above book.

TEEN DADS: Rights, Responsibilities and Joys. Parenting book for teenage fathers.

DETOUR FOR EMMY. Novel about teenage pregnancy.

TOO SOON FOR JEFF. Novel from teen father's perspective.

SURVIVING TEEN PREGNANCY: Choices, Dreams, Decisions For all pregnant teens—help with decisions, moving on toward goals.

SCHOOL-AGE PARENTS: The Challenge of Three-Generation Living. Help for families when teen daughter (or son) has a child.

BREAKING FREE FROM PARTNER ABUSE. Guidance for victims of domestic violence.

DID MY FIRST MOTHER LOVE ME? A Story for an Adopted Child. Birthmother shares her reasons for placing her child.

DO I HAVE A DADDY? A Story About a Single-Parent Child Picture/story book especially for children with only one parent. Also available in Spanish, *¿Yo tengo papá?*

OPEN ADOPTION: A Caring Option A fascinating and sensitive account of the new world of adoption.

PARENTS, PREGNANT TEENS AND THE ADOPTION OPTION. For parents of teens considering an adoption plan.

PREGNANT TOO SOON: Adoption Is an Option. Written to pregnant teens who may be considering an adoption plan.

ADOPTION AWARENESS: A Guide for Teachers, Counselors, Nurses and Caring Others. How to talk about adoption when no one is interested.

TEEN PREGNANCY CHALLENGE, Book One: Strategies for Change; Book Two: Programs for Kids. Practical guidelines for developing adolescent pregnancy prevention and care programs.

MORNING GLORY PRESS
6595 San Haroldo Way, Buena Park, CA 90620
714/828-1998 — FAX 714/828-2049

Please send me the following: Price   Total

Teenage Couples: Caring, Commitment and Change
—	Paper, 0-930934-93-8	9.95	——
—	Cloth, ISBN 0-930934-92-x	15.95	——

Teenage Couples: Coping with Reality
—	Paper, ISBN 0-930934-86-5	9.95	——
—	Cloth, ISBN 0-930934-87-3	15.95	——
— Too Soon for Jeff	Paper, ISBN 0-930934-91-1	8.95	——
—	Cloth, ISBN 0-930934-90-3	15.95	——
—Detour for Emmy	Paper, ISBN 0-930934-76-8	8.95	——
—	Cloth, ISBN 0-930934-75-x	15.95	——
—Teen Dads	Paper, ISBN 0-930934-78-4	9.95	——
—	Cloth, ISBN 0-930934-77-6	15.95	——
—Do I Have a Daddy?	Cloth, ISBN 0-930934-45-8	12.95	——
—Did My First Mother Love Me?	ISBN 0-930934-85-7	12.95	——
—Breaking Free from Partner Abuse	0-930934-74-1	$7.95	——
—Surviving Teen Pregnancy	Paper, 0-930934-47-4	$9.95	——

School-Age Parents: Three-Generation Living
—	Paper, ISBN 0-930934-36-9	10.95	——

Teens Parenting—Your Pregnancy and Newborn Journey
—	Paper, ISBN 0-930934-50-4	9.95	——
—	Cloth, ISBN 0-930934-51-2	15.95	——

Easier Reading Edition—*Pregnancy and Newborn Journey*
—	Paper, ISBN 0-930934-61-x	9.95	——
—	Cloth, ISBN 0-930934-62-8	15.95	——

Spanish—Adolescentes como padres—La jornada . . .
—	Paper, ISBN 0-930934-69-5	9.95	——

Teens Parenting—Your Baby's First Year
—	Paper, ISBN 0-930934-52-0	9.95	——
—	Cloth, ISBN 0-930934-53-9	15.95	——

Teens Parenting—Challenge of Toddlers
—	Paper, ISBN 0-930934-58-x	9.95	——
—	Cloth, ISBN 0-930934-59-8	15.95	——

Teens Parenting—Discipline from Birth to Three
—	Paper, ISBN 0-930934-54-7	9.95	——
—	Cloth, ISBN 0-930934-55-5	15.95	——
—**VIDEO:** "Discipline from Birth to Three"		195.00	——

            TOTAL   ——

Please add postage: 10% of total—Min., $2.50   ——
California residents add 7.75% sales tax   ——

            TOTAL   ——

Ask about quantity discounts, Teacher, Student Guides.
Prepayment requested. School/library purchase orders accepted.
If not satisfied, return in 15 days for refund.

NAME ———————————————————————————

ADDRESS ————————————————————————